Traditional Food

A Taste of Korean Life

KOREA ESSENTIALS No. 4

Traditional Food: A Taste of Korean Life

Copyright © 2010 by The Korea Foundation

First Published in 2010 by Seoul Selection
B1 Korean Publishers Association Bldg., 105-2 Sagan-dong,
Jongno-gu, Seoul 110-190, Korea
Phone: (82-2) 734-9567
Fax: (82-2) 734-9562
Email: publisher@seoulselection.com
Website: www.seoulselection.com

ISBN: 978-89-91913-76-9   04080
ISBN: 978-89-91913-70-7   (set)
Printed in the Republic of Korea

Traditional Food

A Taste of Korean Life

KOREA
FOUNDATION
한국국제교류재단

Seoul Selection

CONTENTS

INTRODUCTION

Diet is one of the most fundamental parts of a people's culture and heritage. It is a collective creation, the product of history and accumulated experience and a reflection of a people's value system. Thus, diets, once established, change surprisingly little over time.

As the final result of much modification and experimentation, traditional food is the most suitable as well as the most nutritious, healthiest, tastiest, and most sanitary for people living in a given condition. Thus, the technique of combining different foods, and of cooking and processing them, can be considered a scientific process. Traditional Korean dietary culture is no different in this respect.

As is the case with other cuisines worldwide, it is difficult to give a precise definition of Korean cuisine. Generally speaking, it developed around rice, without which most Korean meals would be incomplete. The rice is accompanied by a wide variety of communal side dishes—usually, but by no means always, vegetables—and a soup or stew. Of course, there are exceptions to this: Korea also has a wealth of noodle and meat dishes that are served in a multitude of ways. Koreans have shown a particular talent for fermentation, as can be easily seen in Korea's most internationally renowned dish: kimchi. Korea's four seasons and geography have produced a good many seasonal dishes and foods that reflect the nation's geographic characteristics, such as seafood from the ocean that surrounds the peninsula.

Nowadays, with healthy living and the "slow food" movement in the spotlight worldwide, Korean cuisine is drawing major interest as a healthy cuisine with nutritional harmony and balance. In fact,

Koreans have traditionally viewed food as "medicine," a means to keep oneself healthy and strong.

This book will attempt to explore Korea's 5,000-year-old culinary culture and introduce to readers the historical, cultural, nutritional, and philosophical background to this rich cuisine.

"The noted Chicago eatery Blackbird has kimchi on the menu, and California Pizza Kitchen is developing Korean barbecue beef pizza. In Los Angeles, crowds are lining up for street food from a pair of Korean taco trucks called Kogi. The slightly sour-tasting Korean frozen yogurt served at the Pinkberry and Red Mango chains has inspired many imitators... Redolent with garlic, sesame oil and red chili peppers, Korean food is suddenly everywhere."

"The New Hot Cuisine: Korean,"
Wall Street Journal, March 7, 2009

Chapter One

WHY KOREAN FOOD?

Korea's culinary tradition stretches back as long as Korea itself: some 5,000 years. With a history like that, it should come as no surprise that Korean cuisine has developed an incredibly rich and varied menu reflecting the country's unique geographic, climatic, and cultural conditions.

First and foremost, Korean cuisine is balanced and healthy: centered on Korea's staple of rice, the Korean dinner table features an assortment of vegetable and meat dishes prepared in only the most nutritious ways. Indeed, Koreans of old very much regarded food as medicine to keep mind and soul healthy. In these health-conscious days, much attention has focused on the nutritional excellence of Korean food, with no lesser an authority than the World Health Organization praising Korean cuisine as a model of healthy eating. The nourishing quality of Korean cuisine is further enhanced by its use of medicinal herbs to produce a harmony of health and taste.

Korean cuisine is also characterized by its liberal use of fermented foods. Few nations match Korea's variety of fermented dishes and the skill with which dishes are prepared. Korea's internationally best known dish, kimchi, is also its most representative fermented dish. Many of Korea's other better known foods, such as *doenjang* (soybean paste) and *jeotgal* (salted seafood), are also fermented.

Korean food is also vegetable-heavy. While Koreans do eat meat, Korean cooks have taken advantage of the countless vegetables and herbs produced in the country's fertile fields and verdant mountainsides. These vegetables, in turn, are prepared through low-fat "slow food" cooking processes that accentuate taste while preserving nutritional integrity.

Boribap (barley rice), a favorite of Korea's common folk, with mostly vegetarian side dishes. Barley has 16 times the dietary fiber of rice and five times that of flour, and is rich in vitamins and minerals.

THE BALANCED MEAL

The traditional Korean diet consists of balanced, nutritious meals that are made through a variety of cooking methods and techniques developed over generations of experimentation. The main dish of rice, with its accompanying side dishes, provides all the necessary nutrition and taste to keep Korean people healthy. Soup seasoned with spices and grilled foods are shared together with side dishes.

The basic dish is created from a wide variety of ingredients, which combine to form a nutritious, tasty meal. One rule for each meal is that the method of preparation (for example, grilling, frying, or steaming) is not to be repeated, nor are the same ingredients to be used twice. Therefore, the traditional Korean cook has to be very inventive.

Bibimbap, a dish of rice topped with seasoned vegetables and red chili pepper paste, is an increasingly popular dish around the world.

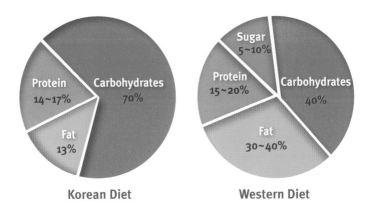

Korean Diet　　　　　**Western Diet**

Koreans also enjoy consuming a good many regional dishes. Korea has four distinct seasons and so produces a variety of different foods depending on the time of year. Korea's plains produce all sorts of grains and vegetables in accordance with the season. At sea, each season produces its own kind of seafood, while the mountains yield ever-changing varieties of mushrooms and mountain herbs. Traditionally, these seasonal foods naturally provide supplementary mineral and nutrient content in accordance with seasonal needs.

With weight and cholesterol problems plaguing much of the developed world, many experiments have been carried out in order to determine the perfect diet. Amazingly enough, many say that Korea has just that diet. The Korean diet has recently been scrutinized by dietitians and research workers because it is found to be well balanced and nutritious.

Whereas in Europe the average diet consists of 40% carbohydrates, 30~40% fat, 15~20% protein and 5~10% sugar, the Korean diet consists of 70% carbohydrates, 13% fat, 14~17% protein, and no sugar; this is considered to be the perfect balance.

LAND OF FERMENTED FOODS

Korean cuisine is most noted for its highly developed culture of fermentation. Fermentation keeps perishable foods fresh and edible for a long time. It preserves and even enhances the nutritional quality of the ingredients. Nutritionally, fermented food has exceptional health effects, reducing cholesterol levels, strengthening the digestive system, and helping prevent cancer. More and more evidence points to the healthiness of eating fermented foods.

Typical Korean fermented foods include soybean-based foods like *doenjang* (soybean paste), *gochujang* (chili paste), *ganjang* (soy sauce), vegetables like kimchi and *jangajji* (pickled vegetables), seafood like *jeotgal* (salted seafood), rice wine, and vinegar. The peculiar nature and character of the taste of Korean food can be explained by the prevalence of fermented food with its own distinctive pungent taste.

Soybean-Based Foods

Soybean-based foods are made by treating soybeans to prepare a variety of products. *Ganjang* is of primary importance in seasoning everything from meat to soup. Whereas Japanese soy sauces include a lot of wheat and are therefore quite sweet, Korean soy sauce is salty and thin. Korean *doenjang* soups taste

"refreshing," as they are light and simple due to the basic nature of the soybean. *Gochujang*, another basic seasoning, makes Korean food very distinctive compared to other types of cuisine. Besides salt, fermented soybean foods include various amino acids and vitamins. Recent research has shown that soy sauce protects the fat in a diet from oxidation. There is some likelihood that soybean foods contain an anti-cancer element, too.

Meju (soybean lumps) drying in a Korean traditional *hanok*. This scene was once common in Korea's farming villages. The blocks are dried until they are hard to the touch; this prevents the breeding of germs.

SECRET OF KOREAN TASTE

When preparing side dishes, *jang* (sauces) are often used to accentuate the taste. The most commonly used sauces are *ganjang* (soy sauce), *doenjang* (soybean paste), and *gochujang* (chili paste). *Ganjang* and *doenjang*, which Koreans have been consuming since ancient times, are seasonings made from soybeans using Koreans' unique fermenting method. Ever since the chili pepper was introduced to Korea during the mid-Joseon Dynasty, chili paste has also been made.

These forms of cooking were considered important as the basic seasoning for food, and a great deal of attention went into taking care of the earthenware jars in which they were stored. Traditional houses had terraces built above the ground for keeping these special storage jars. There was a large jar for soy sauce, a middle-sized one for bean paste, and a small one for chili paste. The jars were kept clean by dusting and polishing them everyday.

MAKING OF *Jang*

To make *jang*, you must first make a *meju* (soybean lump). To do this, the beans are first winnowed, boiled, crushed in a mortar, and shaped into a brick. The brick is then tied up with straw rope and hung up to dry in a warm place for two to three months. The dried brick is washed and put in salt water. The liquid this produces is *ganjang*, while the sediment is turned into *doenjang*.

Meju is made at the end of the tenth lunar month and would be ready to be used by the first lunar month of the following year. Next, it is dried in the sun and made into soy sauce from the end of the first month until early in the third month. An auspicious day is specially picked for making *jang*, and it was customary to avoid the day of *Sinil*, or the "Monkey Day," on which all sorts of activities are avoided.

Making *ganjang* and *doenjang*
The beans are soaked in water, steamed for three to four hours, and molded into *meju*, which are then left to dry. The dried *meju* are put in a clay jar with salt water to make *ganjang*. The mixture is left to mature for 40 to 60 days. Chili pepper and charcoal are added as they have a sterilizing effect. The resulting liquid is *ganjang* and the remaining solid matter is used to make *doenjang*.

Kimchi

Kimchi—originally called *chimchae*, which literally means soaked vegetables—was developed for consumption in circumstances in which fresh vegetables were not available. Thanks to the long Korean winter, making kimchi became a vital yearly routine for every household. Made to retain all the nutrition of fresh vegetables, kimchi can be made from the vegetables of any season. Thus, kimchi has become an essential side dish at any meal in any season and in any place.

Each part of Korea has its own special kimchi; different climates cause the vegetables to ferment to a lesser or greater degree. Kimchi contains various vitamins and minerals. Specially, it is a good source of vitamin C and raw fiber, which helps eliminate constipation and intestinal problems.

It is important to note that chili peppers are the main seasoning used in most Korean dishes. In particular, kimchi and *gochujang* (chili paste) contain a lot of chili pepper powder. The hot element of the chili pepper strengthens the stomach, prevents the oxidation of

Cabbage kimchi, the most common variety of kimchi.

fats, and provides a lot of vitamin C. Because of its sharp, hot taste, kimchi is becoming a popular food around the world (see Chapter 3).

Jeotgal

Jeotgal is a fermented food using salted fish and shellfish. To make *jeotgal*, several sorts of fish, shrimp, and other shellfish are cured in salt and stored. Eventually, the protein ferments and breaks down, producing a unique flavor and aroma. During fermentation the

Kimchi, *jeotgal* and other foodstuffs at a traditional market.

bones grow tender and edible, providing a great source of calcium.

There are about 140 kinds of *jeotgal* in Korea. Some *jeotgal*, like those made from shrimp, anchovies, or other seafood, are generally consumed as seasoning in kimchi, soups, stews, and salads. Other *jeotgal*, like those made of cuttlefish, shellfish, crabs, or oysters are used as side dishes on their own.

VEGETABLE-CENTRIC

Korean cuisine makes wide and varied use of vegetables, mushrooms, seeds and nuts, and seaweed. Most of the foods mentioned above—*doenjang, ganjang, gochujang,* and kimchi—are vegetarian in nature, and vegetables and seaweed are frequently used as *banchan*, or side dishes.

Since Korea's economic rise in the 1970s, Koreans' meat consumption has increased dramatically, but even now Korean cuisine is still focused on vegetables, including soups, side dishes, wraps, and seasoned dishes made from vegetables and seaweed.

Vegetables produced in Korea's mountains and fields are rich in fiber, have antioxidant properties, and have plenty of carotenoids, which boost biological processes. Korean cuisine uses around 10 types of mushroom, including shiitake, manna lichen, oyster mushroom, and tree ear. These mushrooms block the development of bacteria and lower blood pressure.

Rather than using animal fat, vegetable-centric Korean cuisine

makes use of seeds and nuts like sesame, pine nuts, walnuts, and ginkgo nuts to supplement vegetable fats, vitamins, and minerals. Korean dishes frequently use vegetable oils and sesame mixed with salt. Regardless of whether they are prepared raw, steamed, fried, or stewed, a bit of oil and spice is added to heighten the taste. Sesame is a nutritionally outstanding foodstuff, composed of 50% fat and 40% protein. Sesame lowers cholesterol and is high in calcium and iron and well as vitamins B1, B2 and E.

1. Chinese cabbage is needed to make Korea's best known dish, kimchi. It is full of fiber, vitamins, and minerals, including calcium, iron, and vitamin C.

2. Garlic is used in most Korean dishes. In addition to providing a strong aroma, it also cleanses the body of toxic substances, lowers bad cholesterol, stabilizes blood sugar, and restores vigor.

3. Red chili peppers did not come to Korea until relatively recently, but they are now used in so many dishes that they've become a typical ingredient of Korean cooking.

4. Pine nuts are 74% fatty oil and 15% protein, making for a robustly nutritious food. They are used as a garnish in a number of dishes and boiled in *juk* (porridge).

5. Shiitake mushrooms are an oft-used ingredient in Korean cooking, and are utilized in making broths, too. They contain a special component that blocks the buildup of cholesterol in the blood.

6. Sesame plant. The oil from its seed is frequently used in cooking. Mixed with salt, sesame is used as a seasoning and also put into rice cakes, taffy, and cookies.

HEALTHY COOKING METHODS

Low-Fat Cooking Method

Korean cuisine makes frequent use of wet cooking methods with steam or boiled water, as with soups, stews, and sliced meats. Very few dishes are fried in oil. Meat is usually eaten after it has been boiled for a long time, so most of the fat is removed and the caloric content is lowered.

A Slow Food Requiring Effort and Time

Most of the ingredients used in Korean cuisine are not used all at once; rather, they are applied thinly or in layers. Preparing fresh vegetables that are sliced, parboiled, and seasoned, or kimchi and *jeotgal* that are salted and matured, requires a lot of time and effort.

Liberal Use of Seasoning and Spices

Frequently used spices are soy sauce, sugar, green onion, garlic, sesame, sesame oil, and chili pepper. The taste of the spice tends to be strong, overpowering the intrinsic taste of the food, boosting the appetite, and providing a high amount of nutrition. Chili pepper is a seasoning that improves taste and heightens the appetite. Capsaicin—the element in chili pepper that gives it its characteristic spicy kick— helps break down fat, keeping body weight low, and boosts endurance. Garlic, meanwhile, has carbohydrates, phosphorus, sodium, thiamine, and vitamin C.

Food as Medicine

Philosophically, Koreans have traditionally viewed food and medicine as one and the same. Ingredients are chosen in accordance with the principles of *yin* and *yang* and the Five Elements theory so that they benefit the body, while dishes are prepared as if filling a prescription.

Mixing Vegetables and Herbs

Korean cuisine uses a lot of wild mountain vegetables. These vegetables have more nutrients than cultivated vegetables. In particular, they contain many minerals, vitamins, and amino acids. Korean food also uses lots of medicinal herbs like ginseng, licorice, cinnamon, jujube, cassia seed, and acanthopanax.

Samgyetang, or chicken-ginseng soup, is prepared with many herbal ingredients. It's a typical summer dish.

Chapter Two

BASICS OF
KOREAN FOOD

Korea is a peninsula that stretches in a north-south direction from the mainland of Northeast Asia. As a peninsula, it is surrounded on three sides by water, while the land has both plains and mountains, allowing the country to produce a multitude of agricultural goods, seafood, and livestock.

For thousands of years—indeed, until just recently—agriculture was Korea's primary industry, so grain production was of great importance. Of the grains Korea produced, rice was the undisputed king. Korean cuisine typically places a grain (usually rice) as its main dish, surrounded by *banchan* (side dishes) made from vegetables, meat, and/or fish. Unlike Western cuisine, in which each dish—soup, salad, main dish, and dessert—is served on its own plate at its own time, Korean cuisine places all of its dishes on the table at once, where most—including the stews, soups, and *banchan* like the ubiquitous kimchi—are consumed communally.

HARMONY OF *Bap* AND *Banchan*

When Koreans eat, they place several dishes on the table at the same time. This is called *sangcharim*. The Korean *sangcharim* consists of a main dish—usually a bowl of rice (*bap*)—and side dishes (*banchan*) made from various ingredients. Korean cuisine is centered on rice. The *banchan* are considered subsidiary dishes to make the rice more enjoyable. The ingredients used in the *banchan* change from season to season, and while several *banchan* are usually served in a single meal, effort is made to ensure that each one uses different ingredients and cooking techniques.

A typically traditional *sangcharim* (table setting): rice, soup, and sauces accompanied by side dishes of vegetables and meat.

Main Dishes

There is evidence of an agricultural society on the Korean Peninsula from the time of the Neolithic Age. During the Three Kingdom period, rice became a staple of the Korean diet (see p100). There are many ways of cooking rice. It can be boiled alone or with other cereals such as barley, red beans, other beans, and sorghum.

Bap (Rice)

Bap consists mainly of plain white rice, to which other grains are often added. The grains are boiled in water and then well steamed until they are thoroughly cooked. Sometimes, vegetables, seafood, or meat is mixed with the rice. *Bibimbap* is boiled rice mixed with other foods and chili paste.

Juk (Porridge)

To make porridge, whole grains or broken grains are boiled with plenty of water until they are thoroughly cooked and the mixture becomes thick. Vegetables, meat, fish, or shellfish are sometimes added to the mixture. Nuts and beans are also used for porridge, which is mainly eaten for breakfast and as a delicacy and is occasionally offered to people who are sick. Thin rice gruel is made of whole grains of rice boiled in water and then strained.

Guksu (Noodles)

Noodles are usually eaten at lunch time as a simple and light food. Mainly made from the starch of wheat, buckwheat, or arrowroot, noodles can be divided into three different types: warm noodles in hot soup; cold noodles in meat soup or white water kimchi soup; and noodles mixed with vegetables and meat with seasoned sauces.

Manduguk (Dumpling Soup) and *Tteokguk* (Rice Cake Soup)

Dumpling and rice cake soup, like noodles, are served as simple main meals. On New Year's Day, every Korean family prepares *tteokguk* to offer to its ancestors. It has been the first meal of the day since early times. Rice cake soup is made of sliced white rice cakes boiled in meat stock.

Dumpling soup is particularly enjoyed in winter. Dumplings consist of a thin pastry skin, which is filled with a variety of ingredients. The contents include minced meat, kimchi and tofu, bean sprouts and other vegetables, nuts, and seeds.

1
2
3

1. *Juk* (porridge)
2. *Janchi guksu* (banquet-style noodles)
3. *Tteokguk* (rice cake soup)

SIDE DISHES

Rice is always accompanied by subsidiary dishes. Vegetables, meat, fish, and seafood are used as ingredients to make *guk* (soup), *jjigae* (stew), *jeongol* (casserole), *jjim* (steamed dishes), *jorim* (hard-boiled dishes), *gui* (roasted dishes), *jeok* (kebabs), *namul* (seasoned greens), *jangajji* (dried slices of radish or cucumber seasoned with soy sauce), *jeotgal* (fermented seafoods), and kimchi. Soup and kimchi have always been basic requirements for a meal.

In contrast with Western cuisine, where there is little distinction between the main and side dishes, in Korea the side dishes are shared while the main food is served individually. Made to complement the rice, the side dishes also serve as an important source of nutrients. In the side dishes, the taste varies according to the person doing the cooking, though the same ingredients and condiments may be used.

Guk and *Tang* (Soups)

Guk is the most important side dish when the main dish is rice. Soups are divided into clear soups, thick soy bean paste soups, meat stock soups, and chilled soups. They are made with shellfish, vegetables, and seaweed, as well as meat. The meat, anchovy, and kelp are usually used to make the stock, and vegetables are then added to make a good balance. Particularly with meat soup, usually all parts of the animal are used, including the bones, intestines, and blood.

Salt, soy sauce, and chili paste are used to season soup. During the hot summer, chilled soups made of cucumber, seaweed, and sea tangle are often eaten.

| 1 | 3 |
| 2 | |

1. *Kongnamul guk* (bean sprout soup). Reportedly good for hangovers and colds. 2. *Miyeok guk* (seaweed soup). Rich in calcium and iodine, this soup is good for blood circulation, newborn children, and post-natal mothers. 3. *Yukgaejang.* A spicy soup of meat and vegetables, this dish traces its origins to Korean palace cuisine.

Jjigae (Stews)

Jjigae, similar to a Western stew, is served in one common pot and is thicker than soup. *Doenjang jjigae* (soybean stew) is Koreans' favorite stew, with a taste that differs according to the way the soybean paste has been prepared and the ingredients added. The main additions include tofu, zucchini, fresh chilies, beef, anchovies, and various vegetables. *Gochujang jjigae* (chili paste stew) also includes pork, tofu, and many vegetables.

Jeongol (Casserole)

Jeongol is a casserole of seasoned meat, seafood, and vegetables that are fried and then immediately boiled with very little water. It is cooked on a small stove near the table. Specialized restaurants have special tables with a stove in the middle of the table.

1. *Doenjang jjigae* (soybean stew)
2. *Kimchi jjigae* (kimchi stew)
3. *Nakji jeongol* (spicy octopus casserole)

Jjim and *Seon* (Steamed Meat or Seafood)

Korean steaming is done by boiling the food in a soup or by cooking the food in steam. In the former method, meat such as pork or beef is boiled on a small fire for a long time until it is very soft. In the latter method, (usually) fish, shellfish, or shrimp is placed on a steamer. Kimchi *seon* is a kind of *jjim*, the main ingredients of which are kimchi, vegetables, and tofu. The vegetables, which include zucchini, cucumber, anchovies, and eggplant, are boiled or steamed with other minced ingredients, including minced beef.

1. *Domi jjim* (steamed snapper)
2. *Galbi jjim* (steamed beef ribs)
3. *Agu jjim* (steamed angler)

Saengchae (Salad)

Any kind of fresh, seasonal vegetable can be mixed with seasoned soy sauce, chili paste, or mustard to make a salad. Other ingredients include sugar and vinegar, so that the taste is both sour and sweet. Fresh vegetables like radish, lettuce, and cucumber are preferred. Sometimes, salads are made of seaweed, or shellfish such as cuttlefish or shrimp before being mixed with the dressing and vegetables.

Namul (Seasoned Vegetables)

Namul is sometimes called *sukchae*, which means cooked vegetables. It is the most popular Korean side dish, and no meal is complete without as large a variety as the cook has time to prepare. Green vegetables are parboiled and seasoned with various ingredients. Other vegetables like bracken and royal fern are boiled, seasoned, and stir-fried. *Namul* should contain enough sesame oil and sesame powder to be soft

Saengchae and *namul*.

and tasty. Some fresh mountain vegetables are seasoned with chili paste to which vinegar has been added. *Japchae* is a dish of mixed vegetables to which glass noodles and a little beef are added.

Parboiling reduces the bulk of vegetables, and they lose fewer nutrients than with other types of cooking. Sesame oil is used as a seasoning and is the main source of vegetable oil, which helps absorb oil-soluble vitamins. Sesame powder is another nutritious seasoning.

Jorim and *Cho* (Hard-Boiling)

Hard-boiled dishes are mainly shared side dishes. Meat, seafood, and vegetables are boiled and strongly seasoned to create *jorim*, which can be kept for a long time. *Cho* is sweeter than *jorim* and refers to food that has been well boiled initially, with starch paste added to thicken the sauce. The seasoning of *cho* does not need to be as strong as that for *jorim*. The most popular *cho* is made of sea mussels.

Beef jangjorim: Sliced beef marinated in soy sauce. Served as a side dish.

Jeon and *Jijim* (Pancakes)

In these dishes, meat, fish, or vegetables are sliced, seasoned with salt and pepper, and then dipped in flour and egg batter before pan-frying. Pan-fried fish is called *jeonyueo*, and all *jeon* used to be known as *jeonyuhwa* in the royal palace. *Jeonyuhwa* means "flowers pan-fried in oil" and refers to the seasonal flowers that were fried and eaten. *Jeon* was usually cooked in a

Modeumjeon: An assortment of pan-fried foods.

shallow pan. *Jijim* consists of different vegetables mixed with flour and fried in a little oil. Pyeongan-do is famous for pancakes made of ground mung bean paste, and Dongnae in Busan is well known for pancakes made of spring onions and seafood, served sizzling at the table.

Gui and *Jeok* (Broiling and Grilling)

Gui and *jeok* are broiled or grilled foods. Meat, fish, vegetables, and mushrooms are first seasoned or marinated and then put on skewers. *Sanjeok* consists of raw ingredients. After skewering, the food is broiled or grilled. *Nureumjeok* consists of pre-cooked skewered food. *Jijim nureumjeok* is made of raw ingredients, which are skewered and then dipped in flour and egg batter before being cooked.

Top: *Galbi gui* and *seoksoe* (broiled ribs and a gridiron) Bottom: *Haemul sanjeok* (seafood kebab)

Pyeonyuk (Sliced Boiled Meat)

In this dish, a large piece of beef or pork is boiled, covered with a cloth, and pressed. The remaining mass is cut into thin slices and eaten with seasoned sesame sauce or fermented shrimp sauce. The meat used for *pyeonyuk* can come from any part of the animal.

Bossam: Boiled pork, wrapped in a cabbage leaf and eaten, usually with condiments. The pork is often boiled with ginger (to remove the smell) and other medicinal herbs.

Hoe (Raw, Seasoned Fish and Meat)

Hoe is raw or slightly cooked meat or fish that is eaten with seasoned soybean sauce, seasoned chili paste, mustard paste, or an oil and salt mixture. For raw *hoe*, the soft parts of beef or fresh seafood such as croaker, flatfish, pomfret, oyster, or sea cucumber are used. Some kinds of white fish, octopus, squid, and shrimp are parboiled before being served as *hoe*.

Hongeo hoe (fermented skate): A specialty of southwestern Jeolla-do, this dish is high in energy and famous for its powerful aroma.

Jokpyeon and *Muk* (Jelly)

In this dish, the tough parts of beef, such as the leg muscle or skin, are boiled for a very long time. The meat is discarded, and the broth is poured into square vessels and cooled to make *jokpyeon*. The jelly is cut into slices or small pieces and served with seasoned soy sauce.

Muk is made of the starch from the mung bean, wheat, or acorns and is eaten in the same way as *jokpyeon*, sometimes with the addition of vegetables and beef. Seasoned mung bean *muk* is called *tangpyeonchae*.

Cheongpomuk

Twigak and *Bugak* (Fried Flakes)

Twigak consists of roasted dried flakes of kelp, sprouts of tree-of-heaven, or walnuts. *Bugak* is prepared by frying potatoes, chilies, sesame leaves, laver, and leaves of the tree-of-heaven, all of which have been thoroughly dried.

Jangajji (Pickles)

Here, seasoned vegetables are pickled in soy sauce, regular soybean paste, or chili paste. The vegetables include garlic cloves, garlic stalks, sesame leaves, radishes, and cucumber. Just before eating, some of the pickles are cut into slices and seasoned with sesame oil, sesame powder, and sugar.

Various forms of *jangajji* (pickled vegetables).

Po (Beef or Fish Jerky)

Meat *po* is usually made of beef seasoned with soy sauce and then dried. Fish *po* is prepared by drying the whole fish or by drying slices of the flesh seasoned with soybean sauce. Pollock *po* is dried without seasoning.

Jeotgal or *Jeot* (Fermented Seafood)

Jeotgal is made from raw fish, shrimp, or other shellfish mixed with salt and seasoning. The proteins and nucleic acids are hydrolyzed, freeing the amino acids and giving *jeotgal* its peculiar smell and taste. Shrimp *jeot* and anchovy *jeot* are mainly used as minor ingredients for kimchi. *Jeot* made of pollack spawn, cuttlefish, or oysters is used as a side dish.

Myeongnan jeot: Seasoned pollack roe. This dish is also common in Japan, which adopted it from Korea.

Changnan jeot, made from the innards of pollack. This is one of the most popular kinds of *jeotgal* in Korea.

RICE CAKES

Korean rice cakes, *tteok*, are mainly divided into two categories according to the method of cooking. They are either steamed or fried, the latter being first steamed and then fried. *Tteok* can further be divided into two types by the method of preparation: pounded and shaped.

Siru Tteok (Steamed Rice Cakes)

Grains are powdered, mixed, and steamed. There are two kinds of *siru tteok*: with or without layers. *Siru tteok* with layers has powdered red beans, mung beans, or sesame between the layers of rice powder or glutinous rice powder.

Various rice cakes (top to bottom, left to right): *Injeolmi, hwajeon, yeongyang tteok, songpyeon, gyeongdan,* and *siru tteok*

Jeonbyeong (Fried Rice Cakes)

For *Jeonbyeong*, glutinous rice is kneaded in hot water, shaped, and then fried. After it is shaped, seasonal flowers or leaves are placed on top before the cakes are fried to create what are called *hwajeon*.

Shaped cakes, called *juak*, are stuffed with sesame seed powder or Chinese dates mixed with honey. The cakes are shaped into half moons and then fried and served in honey.

Bukkumi is glutinous rice powder or kaoliang powder kneaded in hot water and shaped into a round, thin form, stuffed, and fried.

Injeolmi (Pounded Rice Cakes)

For *injeolmi*, rice or glutinous rice is steamed and powdered, while still hot, in a mortar for a long time. After pounding, it is cut into shapes and rolled in powdered sesame, bean flour, mung bean flour, or other flours. Sometimes, mugwort is added, which gives a natural green color to the cake.

Shaped Rice Cakes

One type of shaped rice cakes, *gyeongdan*, is made from floured glutinous rice dough or kaoliang kneaded in hot water, made into small balls, boiled in hot water, and covered with bean flour or powdered sesame.

Songpyeon is floured rice kneaded in hot water and made into half-moon shapes. These cakes are stuffed with beans, sesame, chopped or powdered chestnuts, or other similar ingredients, and then steamed on a layer of pine needles. *Songpyeon* is made on Chuseok (the harvest festival) (see p79).

Steamed glutinous rice flour or flour that has been kneaded with hot water and then boiled is used for *danja*. The dough is cut or shaped and covered with powdered chestnuts, sliced Chinese dates, or citron.

CONFECTIONERIES

Yakgwa

Yakgwa is made of flour kneaded with sesame oil, honey, wine, and ginger juice before being fried and dipped in honey. There are different kinds of *yakgwa*, which are named according to their size and shape. *Mandugwa* is a kind of *yakgwa* that is stuffed.

Dasik

Powdered grains, herbs, or pollen are kneaded with honey and shaped in a *dasik* frame. Sesame, beans, the angelica plant, pine flower pollen, and flour are also used for *dasik*.

Gangjeong

For this dish, grains are fermented with dried barley sprouts, creating wheat gluten. Roasted beans, sesame, wild sesame, peanuts, raw pine nuts, or ground raw walnuts are mixed with the wheat gluten, which is hardened and cut into small pieces.

Maejakgwa

Maejakgwa or *taraegwa* is a variety of Korean traditional confectionery, consisting of wheat flour, vegetable oil, cinnamon, ginger juice, *jocheong*, and pine nuts.

Yakgwa, dasik, gangjeong, maejakgwa, yugwa, jujube *jeonggwa* and *gwapyeon* (top to bottom, left to right)

Yugwa

Yugwa is divided into various types according to its shape and coating. Powdered glutinous rice is kneaded, shaped, cooked, dried, fried in oil, and covered with various coatings like sesame, black sesame, chopped pine nuts, grains of boiled white rice, or ground grains of glutinous rice. It is then boiled and dried. Ground cinnamon or angelica plant powder is added.

Jeonggwa

To make *jeonggwa*, citron, Chinese quince, ginger, bell flower root, lotus root, or ginseng is boiled in honey malt or sugar.

Suksilgwa

Suksilgwa literally means "cooked fruits." Chestnuts or Chinese dates are boiled in honey. Another method of preparation is to chop chestnuts, Chinese dates, or ginger and, after kneading them into a dough, to make them into shapes. The former and the latter *suksilgwa* are called *cho* and *nam*, respectively.

Gwapyeon

The flesh of sour fruit such as cherries, Chinese quince, or apricots is boiled down in honey, poured into a square vessel, and hardened. It is then cut into slices and served with raw chestnuts or other fresh fruits.

BEVERAGES

Hot beverages are called *cha* (tea), and cold ones are called *hwachae* (punch) or *eumcheong*.

Nokcha (Green Tea)

Nokcha is made of dried tea leaves steeped in hot water. It was introduced during the Three Kingdoms period, at the same time as Buddhism. The habit of drinking *nokcha* declined during the Joseon Dynasty when the national policy was to encourage Confucianism at the expense of Buddhism. Recently, *nokcha* has seen a revival, and the number of people who enjoy drinking it has greatly increased.

Other varieties of tea include those made with barley, Job's tears, corn, brown rice, or wild sesame seeds, which are roasted or pounded and then boiled in water to make tea. Ginseng, ginger, cinnamon bark, the fruits of the *Maximowiczia chinesis* (*Omija*, the five tastes fruit), the Chinese matrimony vine, arrowroot, citron, Chinese quince, and Chinese dates are also used for tea.

Hwachae (Punch)

Hwachae is a beverage based on honey. Rice cakes, glutinous rice cakes, or barley cakes are usually eaten with it. Fruits such as citron, pears, strawberries, mandarin cherries, watermelon, and peaches are also used for *hwachae*.

Sikhye is a unique beverage made from rice that is lightly fermented with dried barley sprouts. *Misu*, or *misutgaru*, consists of ground and roasted mixed grains blended in water with honey or sugar. The yellow pollen of pine tree flowers (*songhwa*) is also mixed in honey to make a drink.

Sikhye

Nokcha

Omijacha

THE TABLE SETTING

A Korean table setting is called a *sangcharim*. On a Korean table, several dishes are placed at once. Broadly speaking, there is a *sangcharim* for normal, everyday meals and a special *sangcharim* for major rites of passage and events.

These everyday *sangcharim* can be further broken down into a *bansang* (usually breakfast and dinner, centered on rice), *juksang* (a simple meal of porridge), *jangguksang* (lunch or simple meals for guests, usually centered on noodles), *juansang* (prepared for drinking alcohol), *gyojasang* (prepared to serve many guests), and *dagwasang* (prepared for tea).

Bansang

Bansang is the usual table of rice, soup, and side dishes. The actual term for it depends on who is doing the eating. For young people, it is called a *bapsang*; for elders, it is called a *jinjitsang*; and for the king, it was called a *surasang*. The setting of the *bansang* varies according to the number of side dishes, starting from three and going up to five, seven,

nine, and twelve. The setting with twelve side dishes was reserved for kings only; this table was called the *surasang* (see p68), which literally means "table offered to the king."

A setting with three side dishes is standard, so let us examine this one as an example. One bowl of rice, a bowl of soup, and a dish of fermented vegetables such as kimchi are placed with three side dishes of vegetable and meat, each cooked differently—either broiled, grilled, deep-fried, or hard-boiled. The ingredients of a meal should be as varied as the method of cooking permits.

Interestingly enough, it used to be that each individual got his own table from which he ate. Now, however, most families gather around a single table to eat together.

Traditional Korean vessels all have different uses. Each one has a special name: *jubal* or *sabal* for rice, *tanggi* for soup, *jochibo* for stews, *kimchibo* for kimchi, and *jongji* for soy sauce or seasoned soy sauce with vinegar. One set of vessels is used for each meal and for each person, and all are of the same material. Ceramic ware is for summer, and silver and brassware, which keep the heat in, are for winter. The contents of each vessel are enough for only one person.

Juksang

Juksang is a table for early morning meals or a simple meal. The main dish is a semi-liquid food like *juk* (porridge) or *mieum* (thin rice gruel). The main dish is arranged with dried side dishes, water kimchi and clear stew. Dried side dishes such as seasoned slices of meat, fish, or salted dry fish are good accompaniments to *juk*.

Insam juk (ginseng porridge)

Noodle soup, rice cake soup, or stuffed dumpling soup is often the main dish for lunch or for a simple meal. Side dishes served include deep-fried fish, a dish of mixed vegetables, kimchi, or white radish water kimchi.

Jangguksang

This was (and still is) prepared for lunch or when holding feasts for guests. The main dish is usually noodle soup (*guksu*), dumplings (*mandu*), or dumpling soup (*manduguk*), served with side dishes such as pan-fried seafood, glass noodles (*japchae*), kimchi, or water kimchi.

When there is a big party for a birthday or a marriage, a large table, called a *goimsang*, is prepared, and a separate table is put in front of the person who is the center of the celebration. This is called an *immaesang*.

Juansang

The *juansang* is prepared to serve wine. The side dishes are chosen according to the type of wine served. Hot soup like *jeongol* and *jjigae*, deep-fried fish, raw fish, seasoned fish or meat, sliced boiled meat (*pyeonyuk*), and kimchi are all suitable.

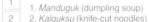

1. *Manduguk* (dumpling soup)
2. *Kalguksu* (knife-cut noodles)
3. *Makgeolli* (liquor made from fermented sweet rice)

Gyojasang

The *gyojasang* is a big table prepared to serve many guests for family celebrations. The main dish is usually noodle soup, rice cake soup, or stuffed dumpling soup, which is scooped out and served in individual bowls. Shared dishes are placed in the middle. The side dishes vary according to the season; possibilities include steamed vegetables, deep-fried fish, sliced boiled meat, broiled or grilled meat or fish, seasoned meat or fish, and vegetables. There should be two kinds of kimchi from among the following: cabbage kimchi, stuffed cucumber kimchi, and white radish water kimchi. For dessert, various confectioneries and a sweet beverage are separately served.

Dagwasang

This is a dessert table prepared for enjoying tea. The tea can be green tea or one of Korea's many medicinal teas, accompanied by rice cakes or other snacks.

After the meal at the wine table or the large table is finished, *dagwasang* is separately prepared. It can also be prepared to serve snacks to guests or visitors. Various rice cakes, confectioneries, and beverages are served.

Dagwasang of tea and snacks

Chapter Three

KIMCHI, KOREA'S STAPLE FOOD

In 2006, the American magazine *Health* designated kimchi as one of the top five healthiest foods in the world, along with olive oil, soy, lentils, and yogurt. In the *Health* article, kimchi was praised for being high in fiber, helpful for dieting, and rich in vitamins A, B, and C, as well as healthful lactobacilli, which are effective for preventing cancer. Moreover, the health benefits of kimchi have been proven in a growing number of scientific studies.

NUTRITIONAL BENEFITS

There are numerous types of kimchi, depending on the ingredients used, but when Koreans mention "kimchi," they are usually referring to Chinese cabbage kimchi, the most common type. With only 32 kcal per 100 grams, kimchi is a low-calorie food, as well as a plentiful source of dietary fiber. Regular intake of dietary fiber helps to prevent constipation, reduce bad cholesterol, and cleanse the body's systems. Kimchi is also a rich source of vitamins and minerals, including vitamin C and beta-carotene, while various B vitamins are synthesized during the fermentation process. It is also high in calcium, iron, and phosphorus, which contribute to strengthened bones and reduced anemia.

Garlic, an essential ingredient of kimchi, contains allicin, a compound with potent antibacterial properties. The global media began to take keen notice when kimchi was cited as one of the factors behind Korea's ability to largely escape the impact of the SARS (severe acute respiratory syndrome) and avian flu outbreaks, which had afflicted certain countries in Asia in recent years. Garlic enables the body to retain vitamin B1 (thiamine) for a longer time, which helps to boost energy and create a sense of calm.

Red chili pepper, which is essential for seasoning kimchi, has a higher content of vitamin C than any vegetable and helps to inhibit the growth of harmful microorganisms, thereby aiding in the production of lactobacilli during fermentation. In fact, the inclusion of red chili pepper significantly bolsters the overall nutritional value of kimchi. When combined with garlic, the two ingredients help to maximize kimchi's anti-cancer effects.

People around the world recognize kimchi as the representative food of Korea.

Good for Dieting?

Kimchi is also ideal for weight control, because it is made primarily from vegetables that are low in calories and high in dietary fiber. Of particular note, capsaicin, the active component of chili pepper, helps to speed up the body's metabolism and burn off fat. The addition of chili peppers to kimchi produces optimal benefits for weight loss; an experiment found that when white mice were fed a high-fat diet together with kimchi, they experienced only minimal weight gain. Moreover, a number of the various microorganisms created during the fermentation process have yet to be carefully studied; the research in this area could result in the discovery of new kimchi-related health and dietary benefits.

Miraculous Fermentation

Kimchi is the result of a natural fermentation process that accounts for its pungent aroma and savory taste, which are enhanced at the peak of its maturity. In addition to the nutritional value of the original kimchi ingredients, the fermentation produces lactobacilli and other nutrients as a result of the interaction of microorganisms. Through a seemingly miraculous fermentation process, which includes the synthesis of lactobacilli, the presence of vitamins B and C and nutrients such as organic acids and amino acids is increased

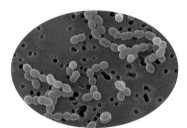

Lactobacilli from kimchi

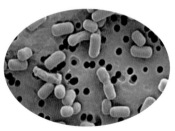

Lactobacilli from yogurt

Seasoned Vegetables' Ability to Block Growth of Stomach Cancer Cells

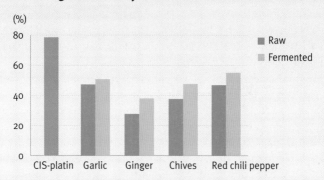

Stomach-Cancer Prevention Effects of Kimchi According to Ripeness

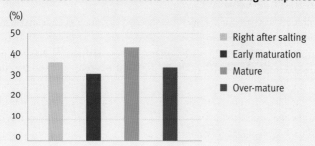

* Using *Leu. mesenteroides*, the bacteria produced by kimchi fermentation, researchers fermented garlic, ginger, red chili pepper, and chives to the maturity level of kimchi (pH 4.2). When applied to stomach cancer cells, they had a cancer growth prevention effect roughly 4% to 10% greater than unfermented garlic, ginger, red chili pepper, and chives.

When CIS-platin, a cancer-fighting agent, and raw and fermented spices were added to stomach cancer cells, the CIS-platin stopped the growth of 79% of the cells. The raw garlic stopped the growth of 47% of the cells, while the fermented garlic prevented the growth of 51% of them. Raw ginger stopped the growth of 29% of the cells, while fermented ginger stopped the growth of 38% of them. Raw chives stopped the growth of 38% of the cancer cells, while fermented chives stopped the growth of 48% of them. Lastly, raw red chili pepper powder stopped the growth of 46% of the cells, while fermented red chili pepper powder stopped the growth of 56% of them.

to far higher levels than in the original ingredients. A single gram of kimchi can contain up to 100 million lactobacilli, a content level four times higher than that of yogurt.

The lactobacilli, lactic acid, acetic acid, and other organic acids produced during the fermentation of kimchi are especially beneficial for the digestive system, relieving constipation as well as inhibiting the growth of mutated cells and the development of tumors in the intestinal tract and thus helping to prevent colon cancer. Also, lactobacilli and organic acids revitalize the skin and create collagen for healthier-looking skin, while functioning as an antioxidant to retard the effects of aging. These nutrients also help to strengthen the immune system and the body's resistance to toxic elements. Of note, the lactobacilli and nutrients in kimchi, as well as its savory taste, reach a peak at the time of its proper fermentation (neither under-fermented nor over-fermented).

Nutritional Composition of Kimchi

Nutrients	per 100 g *
Food energy	32 kcal
Moisture	88.4 g
Crude protein	2.0 g
Crude Lipid	0.6 g
Total sugar	1.3 g
Crude fiber	1.2 g
Crude ash	0.5 g
Calcium	45 mg
Phosphorus	28 mg
Vitamin A	492 IU
Vitamin B1	0.03 mg
Vitamin B2	0.06 mg
Niacin	2.1 mg
Vitamin C	21 mg

* Per 100 g of edible portion.

(Source: Korea Food Research Institute)

Following the SARS outbreak in 2003, kimchi sales in China boomed thanks to talk that the Korean side dish helped prevent the illness. Customers in Beijing sample kimchi at a promotional event held at a large supermarket.

ORIGIN OF KIMCHI

Since prehistoric times, people have used salt as a seasoning and preservative. Kimchi ingredients are allowed to naturally ferment through the formation of lactic acid, a process that has been used to preserve vegetables since the dawn of agricultural cultivation. From its origin as a food preserved with salt, kimchi gradually evolved into its current form through the inclusion of such ingredients as red chili pepper, *jeotgal*, and a variety of seasonings.

The East Asian countries of Korea, China, and Japan all experience cold weather, starting from autumn and continuing into winter. Accordingly, people in the region have long prepared and consumed pickled foods that can be easily stored. In fact, historical documents indicate that pickled foods had become commonplace in the three countries from about the 5th century to the 7th century.

A 5th century Chinese text on agriculture contains detailed records of various preserved foods, while an 8th century Japanese wooden tablet specifying a list of foodstuffs includes references to pickled

The ingredients of kimchi.

cucumbers and pickled rice bran. Interestingly, the recipient of this wooden tablet was a resident of Baekje (18 BC-AD 660). It might be presumed that pickled foods from China crossed the Chinese border into the Korean kingdom of Goguryeo (37 BC-AD 668) and then made their way south into the kingdoms of Baekje and Silla (57 BC-AD 935) before eventually being introduced into Japan.

Taking into account the contextual elements, one can infer that the history of kimchi began during the Three Kingdoms period (1st century BC-AD 7th century) at the latest. A section on "Eastern Peoples" in the Chinese historical text *Records of the Three Kingdoms* mentions: "The people of Goguryeo possess superior technology for brewing liquor, making soy and other sauces, and preparing pickled seafood. Goguryeo plundered the local products of fish and salt from Okjeo [Woju]."

From these accounts, it can be seen that the people of Goguryeo were already aware of the need for salt, an essential ingredient in kimchi, and familiar with the fermentation process. Moreover, the Korean historical text *Historical Record of the Three Kingdoms* (*Samguksagi*, 1145) notes that "Unified Silla Kingdom people enjoyed liquor, soy and other sauces, and pickled seafood at wedding ceremonies in 683," thus confirming the widespread use of foods preserved with salt. Among the relevant relics still around today, there is a stone jar on the grounds of Beopjusa Temple, installed in 720 during the Unified Silla period, which is believed to have been a container for storing kimchi.

Today's Kimchi

The making of kimchi today calls for the basic ingredients of Chinese cabbage, red chili pepper, and *jeotgal*. Chinese cabbage is the primary component of kimchi, which is seasoned with red chili and *jeotgal*. Nonetheless, it was not until the 17th century that Chinese cabbage, red chili, and *jeotgal* became the primary ingredients of kimchi. It was during the 200 year period from the late 17th century to the late 19th century that a wide variety of vegetables and seasonings, such as red chili, green onion, garlic, ginger, and *jeotgal*, were first used to make kimchi.

Chinese cabbage has been cited in medical texts as a vegetable with medicinal benefits. It appears to have been widely cultivated from the mid-16th century and was likely used for the making of kimchi. Red chili is thought to have been introduced from Japan around the time of the Japanese invasions of Korea (1592-1598). A record from 1613 states "Red chili pepper has been brought over from Japan, and it is poisonous." However, it was not until sometime later that red chili pepper became an ingredient of kimchi, because of a lack of awareness of its usefulness as a seasoning.

The key factors that led to the inclusion of red chili pepper in kimchi were related to the development of agricultural technology and the occurrence of natural phenomena, such as floods and droughts, which resulted in serious food shortages. Based on a 1765 account, which noted, "These days, red chili pepper is being cultivated in large amounts, and appearing in the market in large amounts as well," it seems that red chili pepper was widely used in the 18th century.

Various forms of kimchi (top to bottom, left to right): radish kimchi, white kimchi, sliced radish kimchi, cabbage kimchi, cucumber kimchi, and water kimchi made of sliced radish.

The first reference to the use of cabbage and red chili pepper in kimchi is found in the *Supplement to Forestry Administration* (*Jeungbo Sallimgyeongje*, 1766), which included recipes for making some 20 varieties of kimchi, including cabbage kimchi. The *Women's Quarters Series* (*Gyuhap Chongseo*, 1809) also explained how to season kimchi with *jeotgal*. Various types of preserved seafood had been around since the Three Kingdoms period, but it was only in the mid-1700s that it began to be used to make kimchi. It was also found that the addition of preserved seafood allowed the amount of salt to be reduced.

By the early 18th century, the making of kimchi included Chinese cabbage, red chili pepper, garlic, and *jeotgal*, resulting in a form similar to the popular varieties of today. Yet there are countless variations of kimchi, based on the ingredients used and the region of its preparation, along with the continuous adoption of innovative twists. Kimchi, which remains deeply rooted in Korea's everyday lifestyle, might well lead the way in efforts to globalize Korean food.

SHARING KIMCHI AROUND THE WORLD

Today, there is no doubt that people around the world recognize kimchi as the representative food of Korea. Even if they might not have actually tasted kimchi, it is the first thing they think of at the mention of Korean food. Nowadays, kimchi is regularly consumed in 40 or so countries worldwide. And in line with the fast-growing interest in kimchi around the world, Korea has been pursuing the international standardization of kimchi since 1994.

This effort has led to the adoption, in July 2001, of standards for Chinese cabbage-based kimchi by the Codex Alimentarius Commission, an international organization that oversees the establishment of international standards for specified foods. Kimchi is thus the first traditional Korean food to formally acquire such international recognition, which includes an acknowledgement that Korea is the originator of kimchi. More recent milestones in the globalization of kimchi include the launch of Korea's first-ever astronaut into space along with kimchi provisions (February 2008).

Global Kimchi Market

In Korea, about 150,000 tons of kimchi are produced and consumed annually. Of this amount, 70 percent, or some 100,000 tons, is Chinese cabbage kimchi, confirming its status as the favorite variety in Korea, and the best-known type among foreigners as well. The remaining 30 percent is made from a variety of vegetables, such as white radish, young radish, and mustard leaf. Based on retail sales, the Korean kimchi market is valued at about 5 trillion won (about $5 billion) on an annual basis, involving the production of some 600 kimchi manufacturers.

According to a survey by the Korea Agro-Fisheries Trade Corporation, the kimchi market outside of Korea is valued at an estimated $1 billion per year. Of this amount, about 10 percent, or $100 million, is produced in Korea, with Japan being the number one importer of Korean-made kimchi. Japan's kimchi market in 2008 reached some 66 billion yen (about $700 million), indicating that Korean-produced kimchi accounts for only a 20 percent share of the Japanese market. It is estimated that about 300 kimchi makers currently operate in Japan, of which about 50 firms market their products through large-scale distribution companies. This clearly shows that kimchi making, after being introduced from Korea, has become a thriving industry in Japan.

In addition to Japan, countries in which kimchi is readily available include Taiwan, the United States, and China, each of them maintaining an annual kimchi market of about $100 million. The current share of Korean-made kimchi in the Taiwanese market is about 10 percent, while that in the US market is a mere 5 percent.

On the other hand, China exports about 95 percent of the kimchi it produces, primarily to Korea and Japan. In recent years, the global kimchi market has been enjoying steady annual growth. However, the global market share of Korean-produced kimchi is quite insignificant, even though Korea is the originator of kimchi.

Promotional Efforts

Kimchi festivals, both large and small, are regularly held in Korea, with the best-known being the Kimchi Love Festival in Seoul and the Gwangju Kimchi Festival in Gwangju. Moreover, these events offer an overview of the historical evolution of kimchi from the Three Kingdoms period (1st century BC-AD 7th century) through the Joseon period (1392-1910) and provide samples of rare kimchi

Foreigners make kimchi at Namsangol Hanok Folk Village in Seoul.

varieties with which many people are unfamiliar, such as the kimchi specially prepared for temple life, ancestral rituals, and ancient palaces. In addition, there are also fusion dishes that combine kimchi with foods from around the world in a bid to pique the interest of foreigners. At the various international food exhibitions held in Korea, kimchi tasting and product displays are supplemented by a variety of hands-on activities, such as kimchi making sessions and demonstrations of the preparation of kimchi-related dishes, which provide Koreans and visitors from abroad with first hand experiences with the preparation and uses of kimchi.

The government is actively pursuing a number of efforts to promote the globalization of kimchi, including public relations activities and marketing initiatives focused on boosting kimchi exports. For example, the Ministry of Food, Agriculture, Forestry, and Fisheries launched a comprehensive publicity program in 2007 for the purpose of introducing the world to the delectable foods of Korea, which included the publication of *300 Beautiful Korean Foods,* a book containing standardized recipes for favorite Korean dishes. In particular, it provides 14 recipes for various types of kimchi, which include step-by-step instructions that can be easily followed by people with little or no familiarity with Korean food.

Standardization of Kimchi

There are countless variations of noncommercial kimchi, which vary according to the ingredients and seasonings and the fermentation process, as well as the personal preferences of a family or residents of a particular region. For commercially produced varieties as well, the different factors that are involved with the making of kimchi can result in certain variations in taste and appearance. However, to gain wider consumer acceptance it is necessary for kimchi manufacturers to offer a product with a consistent quality and taste, for which the standardization of kimchi is essential.

For some time now, the Korean government has been conducting extensive research on this matter, which has resulted in a standardization proposal for assessing the spiciness and extent of fermentation of kimchi. In this regard, spiciness is defined through five levels, depending on the amount of capsaicin (the active component of red chili pepper), and Scoville ratings to measure hotness: mild, slightly hot, moderately hot, very hot, and extra hot. The extent of fermentation, which depends on the length of the maturation period, can now be regulated better as a result of recent advances in temperature control during the distribution process.

Based on the pH level and overall acidity, three levels of fermentation have been established to measure sourness: nonfermented, moderately fermented, and highly fermented. Under this system, consumers can select from among 15 combinations of kimchi spiciness and fermentation based on their individual tastes. Standardization of the spiciness and fermentation of kimchi products will help to bolster appeal among a broader range of consumers both at home and abroad. In this way, the standardization of kimchi will help to pave the way for the globalization of kimchi and the continued development of the kimchi making industry.

Path to Globalization

The development of kimchi fusion dishes and the availability of a wide variety of kimchi products will be instrumental for attracting a broad base of consumers who are not well acquainted with Korean food. Fortunately, the combination of kimchi with Western cuisine has already gained considerable popularity. In particular, kimchi is an ideal complement to dishes including cheese such as spaghetti, gratin, and tortillas, due to the fact that it provides an added crispness to the overall flavor and serves to offset any greasiness.

Other fusion dish creations include kimchi with rice croquettes, spring rolls, and tofu burgers, while there are numerous dishes that feature a kimchi puree sauce. In addition, food researchers are continuously devising kimchi with new flavors, appearances, and colors in order to change existing attitudes toward the dish. Examples of specialty types include good-health kimchi, such as versions made with broccoli, fruit extract, and ginseng, along with novel kimchi products such as kimchi essence-infused chocolate, cake, and pudding.

Kimchi is undergoing rapid change inside and outside of Korea. In Japan, where kimchi is firmly rooted in the local food culture, the combination of kimchi and Japanese foods has led to the creation of many new dishes. In fact, a growing number of Japanese restaurants

French dishes using kimchi at a fusion kimchi tasting event hosted by the French cooking school Le Cordon Bleu and Sookmyung Academy.

now offer such kimchi-based items as *norimaki*, sushi, *soba*, *misoshiru*, *nabe*, and broiled eel rice.

Also noteworthy is the integration of kimchi into French cuisine at France's Le Cordon Bleu, one of the world's foremost culinary institutes, where 20 French-style kimchi dishes have been developed, including fried kimchi and Camembert, kimchi-salmon cannelloni, and kimchi-cauliflower soup. The recipes for these dishes have been published and are taught at 26 Le Cordon Bleu affiliate institutes in 15 countries.

Meanwhile, active research efforts are being undertaken to develop specialty kimchi products that are effective for the treatment of various diseases. The Korea Food Research Institute has joined forces with university research teams to pursue a variety of research initiatives in this regard. In November 2007, they developed a high-function kimchi with an S-adenosyl methionine (SAM) content three times higher than that of regular kimchi.

SAM, a natural biological element, is known to be helpful for mitigating the effects of liver toxicity, depression, neurological disease, dementia, arthritis, and high cholesterol. In March 2008, another high-function kimchi was developed that increased the level of gamma-aminobutyric acid (GABA), a neurotransmitter amino acid that has been shown to be effective in improving blood flow to the brain, relieving stress, improving memory, reducing blood pressure, alleviating depression, and relieving insomnia.

Chapter Four

SPECIAL & LOCAL VARIETIES

Korean cuisine has developed its own flavors and character according to region and class. In the highly stratified society of the Joseon Dynasty (1392-1910), each social class developed its own culinary culture. The royal court had its cuisine, the elite *yangban* class had its own cuisine, and the commoners had their cuisine. Religion also played a factor, with Buddhists developing a unique Buddhist temple cuisine.

The result has been an incredibly varied cuisine, despite Korea's relatively small size. In modern times, these various cuisines have transcended their original class, religious and regional boundaries, and can now be enjoyed by most everyone everywhere, although regional dishes are still best enjoyed in their regions of origin. Buddhist cuisine, too, is probably best enjoyed in the peaceful serenity of Korea's Buddhist monasteries, though restaurants specializing in Buddhist cooking can be found even in the heart of Seoul.

SPECIAL CUISINES

Banga Cuisine

Banga cuisine is the food of the *yangban*, the scholar elites that dominated Korean society in the Joseon era. It is characterized by "family foods" passed down through the generations, with plenty of regional variation. When *yangban* took government posts, they would come up to Seoul, but they would never forget their hometown food, so each *yangban* house had its own special dishes. The *yangban* also took cues from palace cuisine, developing in their food a unique taste and style that would become known as *hyangto* (local) food.

As *yangban* cuisine differed from house to house and region to region, it was usually passed down by the wives in the family. This became the model of Korean cuisine, with many traditional dishes preserved thanks to Confucian ideology.

Traditional *bangasang*. Each dish is covered to keep it warm.

Palace Cuisine

Korean royal palace cuisine, as the name would suggest, was the style of Korean cooking traditionally reserved for the court of the Joseon Dynasty. With the fall of the dynasty and the end of the monarchy, palace cuisine almost became a lost art, but it was preserved by a few chefs who kept the cuisine going, mostly at private restaurants for high-end clients. In the 21st century, it has witnessed a revival, its popularity boosted by popular media and the so-called Korean Wave, which has brought the beauty of Korean palace cuisine to media markets in China, Japan, and elsewhere in Asia.

Korean palace cuisine reflected the grandeur and flair of Korea's kings of old. Palace cuisine served as a national showcase: the king's dinner table featured dishes from all over the Korean Peninsula, as well as surrounding nations. Each region in Korea sent its local specialties to the palace for the king to consume. Unlike commoners, whose food was seasonal, the king's dinner table

Reenactment of Joseon queen's 60th birthday.

changed day to day. Accordingly, each month the governors of Joseon's eight provinces presented the court with their local ingredients, giving palace chefs an incredible wealth of ingredients with which to work.

Food was taken very seriously by the Joseon government. Government ministries included positions dedicated to the procurement of food and drink for the royal family. For example, the Ministry of Personnel contained positions responsible for obtaining rice for royal consumption. The Ministry of Rites prepared sacrificial foods for ancestral rites, and procured alcoholic beverages and medicinal foods. Within the palace, there were countless servants and court maids who prepared dishes such as tofu, alcoholic beverages, tea, and rice cakes. The court maids in particular served as the palace cooks, serving with government bureaus such as the Bureau of Special Food and Bureau of Cooking Food. During major banquets, the female cooks might be assisted by male cooks from outside the palace.

Top: *Gujeolpan* is a dish consisting of nine different foods served on a wooden plate with nine sections.

Bottom: *Sinseollo*, a variety of *jeongol*, is boiled in meat stock with various vegetables and mushrooms in a particular type of cooking pot with holes.

During the Joseon Dynasty, five meals a day were served in the royal palace. Of these, two were full-course meals, while three—the pre-breakfast, afternoon, and after-dinner meals—were lighter. These meals were:

- *Mieumsang* (**Pre-breakfast**): The first meal of the day, this was served to the king and queen at sunrise and usually consisted of rice porridge (*juk*) made from abalone, white rice, mushrooms, pine nuts, and sesame. The porridge was often accompanied by side dishes like kimchi, oysters, and soy sauce. This meal was thought to boost the royal couple's vitality.

- *Surasang* (**Full-course**): Breakfast and dinner were the two main meals of the day and consisted of two types of rice, two types of soup, two types of stew, a dish of steamed meat, a casserole, three types of kimchi, three sauces, and 12 side dishes. These were served in a special dining room, with the king seated to the east and the queen to the west, attended by court maids. Typically, the meal was served with three tables and a hot pot. The largest table would be placed at the bottom left (from the king's perspective); this contained the rice, soups and stews, and side dishes. A smaller table would be placed at the bottom right; this would contain thicker meat soups and desserts, as well as provide a place to put empty bowls. Sauces, raw vegetables, eggs, and sesame oil would be placed on a table at the upper right. Finally, a heated hot pot table would hold the casserole (see p68).

- *Natgeonsang* (**Afternoon**): Lunch was usually a simple affair of porridge, but when guests came they were usually treated to noodles and dumplings.

- *Yachamsang* (**After-dinner**): A simple evening snack was sometimes served to the king and queen as well.

DAE JANG GEUM

The popular Korean drama *Dae Jang Geum* starring actress Lee Young-ae, told the tale of a palace cook in the Joseon era. A hit in China and other Asian markets, the show provided a look at Korean palace cuisine and the culture that surrounded it.

Loosely based on the historical figure during the reign of King Jungjong (r. 1506-1544) as depicted in the *Annals of the Joseon Dynasty*, the show focuses on Jang-geum (played by Lee), the first female royal physician of the Joseon Dynasty. The main themes are her perseverance and the portrayal of traditional Korean culture, including royal court cuisine and traditional medicine.

Dae Jang Geum enjoyed extensive success throughout Asia, in places such as China, Taiwan, Hong Kong, Malaysia, Singapore, Brunei, Japan, Indonesia, the Philippines, Thailand, and Vietnam, further continuing the "Korean Wave" cultural fever that has gripped Asia since the early 2000s. It has also been shown in Australia, the United States, Sweden, Russia, Iran, Saudi Arabia, Turkey, Peru, Egypt, Romania, Canada, India, Israel, Hungary, and New Zealand. *(Adapted from Wikipedia)*

Musical version of the hit Korean Wave drama *Dae Jang Geum*,

SURASANG SETTING

Side Table 2
(*Chaeksangban*)

Casserole, *doenjang* soup,
meat, sesame oil, eggs, and
vegetables

The King's Dietary Routine

A king's dining culture differed from other people's, beginning with the number of meals. The king ate five times a day, although of these, two of them—the morning and evening meals—were *surasang*, or full meals. These meals consisted of the best foods, but, contrary to what one might suspect, little oil was added, and most of the dishes were rather bland in taste.

The morning *sura* was served at 10 am, while the evening *sura* was served at 5 pm. Ten in the morning is the time when the positive energy is at its most abundant, while 5 pm is right before the energy of the day is up. Accordingly, if one consumes food at these times, digestion, absorption, and storage run smoothly.

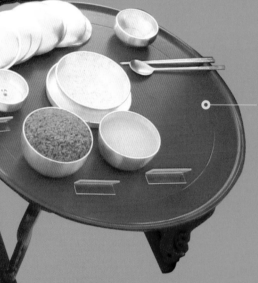

Side Table 1
(Gyeotban)

Pat sura (rice mixed with red bean), bowl for scorched rice tea, three silver bowls, and three silver plates

Main Table *(Wonban)*

White rice, seaweed soup, stew, steamed meat or fish, casserole, three types of kimchi, three sauces, and 12 side dishes including *jeotgal*, sliced steamed meat, raw fish or beef or fermented raw fish, poached egg, seasoned vegetables, salad, grilled meat or fish, pancakes, *jangajji* (fermented vegetables in soy sauce), jerked meat or seafood, *jorim* (food boiled in seasonings)

Temple Cuisine

Korean temple cuisine is a reflection of the basic spirit of Buddhism. Dishes are kept simple, while ingredients are kept as pure as possible, allowing their intrinsic tastes to shine.

In accordance with Buddhist principles, temple cuisine does not use meat, nor does it use the *osinchae*, or "five stimulating seasonings" (garlic, green onions, wild chives, regular chives, and *heunggeo*), giving temple cuisine a simple, pure taste.

For ingredients, temple food uses mountain vegetables, field vegetables, roots, berries, bark, and seaweed. The cooking process is simple and designed to preserve as much as possible the original taste of the major ingredients. Accordingly, artificial seasoning is kept to a bare minimum. It's an odd contradiction that Buddhism, which seeks to minimize our appetites, has at the same time elevated the taste of its food to untold heights.

Until recently, this cuisine was the preserve of temples sheltered from the mundane world. Now, however, opportunities to experience this cuisine are expanding, especially as vegetarianism continues to grow in popularity as a healthy alternative.

Menu at a Korean temple cuisine restaurant in Insa-dong. The table is covered with vegetables, salads, fried goods, and *doenjang* stew.

LOCAL CUISINES: SOUTH KOREA

The Korean Peninsula stretches in a north-south direction from the Northeast Asian mainland and is surrounded by water on three sides. Accordingly, the topographic and climactic conditions found throughout the peninsula are quite diverse, producing a wide variety of *hyangto* (local) foods. Each province produces a great many dishes unique to its locality. In the 20th century, however, the development of national transportation, ease of delivery, and a widening distribution net have had an impact on local cuisine.

Seoul

Seoul itself doesn't produce much agriculturally, but it takes ingredients from throughout the country to produce a wide variety of succulent dishes. Among Korean cities, Seoul, Gaeseong, and Jeonju have the most diverse and eye-catching local cuisines.

As it was the capital of the Joseon Dynasty for 500 years, Seoul still maintains many of the culinary traditions of the period, including its preference for mild dishes that are neither spicy nor salty. Home to many royals and *yangban*, Seoul was quite strict about its culinary rules and placed a lot of emphasis on presentation. **Dishes:** *Sinseollo* (royal casserole), *gujeolpan* (nine-sectioned plate), *seolleongtang* (beef soup), *yukgaejang* (spicy beef soup), *galbi jjim* (braised meat short ribs)

Gyeonggi-do

With rich fishing grounds to the west and plenty of wild mountain vegetables in the east, Gyeonggi-do produces a wide variety of foodstuffs, including rice and dry-field agricultural goods. Dishes tend to be simple and many, and presentation is pleasantly plain, with the exception of Gaeseong, which was incorporated into North Korea after the Korean War. In Gaeseong, the old royal capital of Goryeo, the cooking style is quite sumptuous (see p105). **Dishes:** *Galbi* (grilled short ribs), *samgyetang* (chicken-ginseng soup), *kongguksu* (cold soybean noodle soup), *ogokbap* (steamed five cereal crops), Gaeseong: *joraengi tteokguk* (Gaesong style rice cake soup), *bossam kimchi* (wrapped kimchi), *gyeongdan* (ball-shaped rice cake), *chueotang* (mudfish soup)

Gangwon-do

With its many mountains and high plains, Gangwon-do produces a lot of corn, buckwheat, and potatoes; accordingly, it produces many dishes using these ingredients. The East Sea, meanwhile, produces pollack, squid, and seaweed, a fact well represented in local cuisine.
Dishes: *Makguksu* (buckwheat noodle), *gamjajeon* (potato pancake), *ojingeo sundae* (blood sausage stuffed with squid), *myeongnan jeot* (seasoned pollack roe)

Chungcheong-do

One of Korea's primary agricultural regions, Chungcheong-do produces large amounts of rice, barley, sweet potatoes, radishes, cabbage, cotton, and ramie. Its west coast, meanwhile, produces much seafood. Since the days of the Baekje Kingdom, the region has produced a good deal of rice. Its local dishes are quite simple in presentation, representing the simple manners of the local residents.

Chungcheong-do residents have traditionally enjoyed *doenjang*; in winter, they like heartier soups like *cheonggukjang*. Locals tend to go easy on spices, instead preferring to let the natural taste of the food come through. The local cuisine is simple and plain-tasting, in sharp contrast to the cuisines of Gyeongsang-do and Jeolla-do.
Dishes: *Kalguksu* (knife-cut noodle soup), *jeyuk bokkeum* (stir-fried pork in gochujang) *kongnamul bap* (rice cooked with sprouts), *cheonggukjang jjigae* (fermented soybean stew)

Jeolla-do

Possessing perhaps the most famous of Korea's local cuisines, Jeolla-do produces a wide variety of grains, seafood, and wild vegetables compared to other regions, and the food it produces is especially

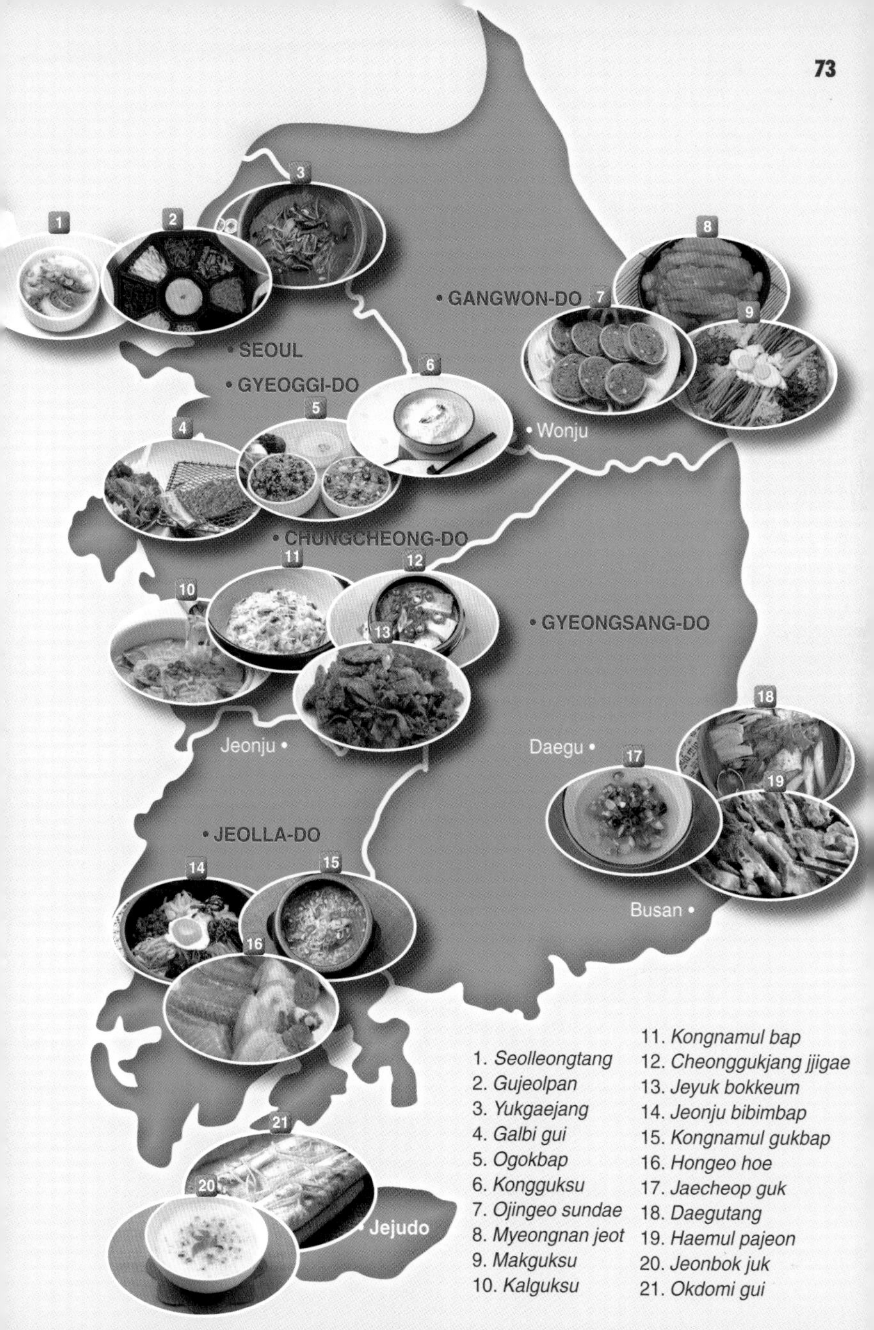

GANGWON-DO
SEOUL
GYEOGGI-DO
Wonju
CHUNGCHEONG-DO
GYEONGSANG-DO
Jeonju
Daegu
JEOLLA-DO
Busan
Jejudo
1
2
3
4
5
6
7
8
9
10
11
12
13
14
15
16
17
18
19
20
21

1. *Seolleongtang*
2. *Gujeolpan*
3. *Yukgaejang*
4. *Galbi gui*
5. *Ogokbap*
6. *Kongguksu*
7. *Ojingeo sundae*
8. *Myeongnan jeot*
9. *Makguksu*
10. *Kalguksu*
11. *Kongnamul bap*
12. *Cheonggukjang jjigae*
13. *Jeyuk bokkeum*
14. *Jeonju bibimbap*
15. *Kongnamul gukbap*
16. *Hongeo hoe*
17. *Jaecheop guk*
18. *Daegutang*
19. *Haemul pajeon*
20. *Jeonbok juk*
21. *Okdomi gui*

extravagant. In localities like Jeonju, Gwangju, and Haenam, wealthy noble families have lived together, handing down within households good foods with incomparable style and taste. While Gaeseong in Gyeonggi-do has been quite conservative in its culinary culture, protecting the cuisine of the Goryeo Dynasty, Jeolla-do has kept the culinary traditions of Joseon. It uses ingredients well, producing a wide range of dishes. The bean sprouts of Jeonju are particularly noted for their flavor.

Jeolla-do cuisine is famous for filling the table with a lot of side dishes; this can surprise first-time visitors to the region. Bordering both the South and West Seas, the region produces many kinds of unique seafood products and *jeotgal*. Due to the warm weather, the flavors tend to be spicy and provocative, with liberal use of *gochujang* (chili paste). **Dishes:** *Jeonju bibimbap* (mixed rice of Jeonju), *kongnamul gukbap* (soybean sprout soup with rice), *hongeo hoe* (fermented skate), *kkaejuk* (sesame porridge)

Gyeongsang-do

Gyeongsang-do has good fisheries to the south and east, so it is rich in seafood and it has rich farmland on the banks of the Nakdonggang River. Its dishes tend to be salty and spicy, but not as extravagant as Jeolla-do cuisine. Residents also like to salt fresh fish and boil fish stews. **Dishes:** *Daegutang* (cod stew), *miyeok honghap guk* (seaweed soup with mussel), *haepari hoe* (raw jelly fish), *haemul pajeon* (seafood pancake), *jogae jjim* (steamed seashells), *jaecheop guk* (a clear soup made with small freshwater clams)

Jeju-do

Jeju-do produces hardly any rice, but it produces a lot of beans, barley, millet, and sweet potatoes. It is especially famous for its mandarin oranges and abalone.

Jeju-do dishes use a lot of fish and seaweed (not surprising, given that it's an island), and locals use *doenjang* to season dishes. They also enjoy fish stews and porridge.

Jeju-do residents reflect their native industry and simplicity in their dishes: they rarely mix many ingredients together, and they don't use much seasoning. Dishes tend to be on the salty side. Also unsurprisingly, they eat a lot of raw fish. **Dishes:** *Jeonbok juk* (abalone porridge), *okdom juk* (tilefish porridge), *okdom gui* (grilled tilefish)

LOCAL CUISINES: NORTH KOREA

Pyeongan-do

Pyeongan-do cuisine is characterized as a continental style due to a lot of interaction with China dating back to ancient times. Dishes are made into large shapes, so the table looks rich and abundant. *Jobap*, a bowl of mixed steamed rice and millet, is commonly served in place of *ssalbap* (steamed rice without any other grains), and foods made with grain flour such as noodle dishes—especially *naengmyeon* (cold buckwheat noodles)—and *mandu* (dumplings) are common Pyeongan dishes. The cuisine's taste is generally bland, with fatty foods being enjoyed during winter. **Dishes:** *Dwaejigogi jeon* (pork pancakes), *dongchimi* (water kimchi), *baek kimchi* (kimchi seasoned without chili pepper powder), *mujigae tteok* (rainbow rice cake)

Pyongyang

Pyongyang, the capital of North Korea, was the capital of Gojoseon, and the provincial capital of Pyeongan-do until 1946. Therefore, Pyongyang cuisine shares the general culinary tradition of Pyeongan-do. The most famous local food is Pyongyang *naengmyeon*, also called *mul naengmyeon*. *Naengmyeon* literally means "cold noodles," while the affix *mul* refers to "water," as the dish is served in a cold soup. **Dishes:** Pyongyang *naengmyeon* (cold buckwheat noodle soup), *eobok jaengban* (pressed beef served in a brass plate), Pyongyang *manduguk*

1. *Baek kimchi*
2. *Sundae*
3. *Injeolmi*
4. *Myeongnan jeot*
5. *Mujigae tteok*
6. *Japgokbap*
7. Hamhung *naengmyeon*
8. Pyongyang *naengmyeon*
9. Pyongyang *manduguk*
10. *Sundubu jjigae*
11. *Cheongpomuk*

• HAMGYEONG-DO

• PYEONGAN-DO

Hamheung •

• PYONGYANG

• HWANGHAE-DO

Haeju •

• GANGWON-DO

• Seoul

Hamgyeong-do

Hamgyeong-do lies in the far northern region of the Korean Peninsula, comprising steep mountains and valleys while facing the East Sea. Cereal crop farming is developed in the region, so a diverse range of high-quality cereals is harvested, including millet, barnyard millet, sorghum, soybeans, and corn. The quality of potatoes and corn is also high, so the starch obtained from these crops is used to make noodles. Although Hamgyeong-do cuisine is not salty, garlic and chili pepper are heavily used as seasonings. Hamhung *naengmyeon*, which originates in the city of Hamhung, is a cold noodle dish topped with *hoe* (sliced raw fish) seasoned with a hot and spicy sauce. **Dishes:** *japgokbap* (a bowl of cooked mixed multiple grains), *jjin jobap* (steamed sorghum), *dak bibimbap* (mixed rice and vegetables with chicken slices), *eollin kongjuk* (porridge made with frozen soybeans), *oksusu juk* (corn porridge), Hamhung *naengmyeon, gamja guksu* (potato noodles)

Hwanghae-do

Hwanghae-do is a granary of North Korea and is known for its production of good-quality cereal. The abundant production of cereal crops leads to a higher quality of feed for livestock, so the quality of meat produced in the region is said to be good. Chickens are raised in every household, and the meat is fleshy and of good quality, so it is used for many dishes in Hwanghae-do cuisine. Chicken is used as an ingredient in wheat noodle dishes and *mandu* (dumplings). Due to the climate, the kimchi of the Hwanghae region has a clear and refreshing taste, so its brine is used as a soup on many occasions. Hwanghae-do dishes are savory and simple, with less decoration. The most famous Hwanghae-do dish is Haeju *bibimbap*, originating in the city of Haeju. **Dishes:** Haeju *bibimbap*, *japgokbap* (rice with multiple grains), *sundubu jjigae* (spicy soft tofu stew, *bindaetteok* (mung bean pancake), *cheongpomuk* (seasoned mung bean starch jelly)

Chapter Five

HOLIDAYS, CEREMONIES & FOOD

In all cultures, cuisine can be classified into two different categories: everyday food and occasional food. Everyday food refers to the food eaten daily during meals. It is usually simple, wholesome, and not very expensive. Occasional food refers to anything eaten as a snack or a delicacy, as well as the food consumed during special holidays or festivals and at ritual ceremonies. This food is usually more expensive, more difficult to prepare, particular to a specified occasion and much loved by the people.

In Korea, the daily fare is simple. Consisting mostly of plain rice, a soup, and a few side dishes, the menu follows the seasons carefully. Festival food, on the other hand, is far more complicated and intricate. Traditionally, everyone looked forward to holidays because they were times when special food was served in order to celebrate a special day and effectively supplement the regular diet.

HOLIDAY FOOD

Whereas plain boiled rice is central to daily dishes, it is not so with holiday dishes. When rice is served during holidays, it is usually glutinous rice or some other unusual form. Rice cakes, red bean porridge, and glutinous rice are some of the main items in an occasional dish. During ancestral memorial services or at parties, ordinary rice is consumed along with many special food items, such as rice cakes, fruits, and various side dishes.

Traditionally, the food eaten during holidays is determined by the occasion, the season, and the customs. For example, on New Year's Day (Seollal), rice cake soup called *tteokguk* is served. Consisting of broth with thinly sliced rice cakes, *tteokguk* is believed to grant the consumer luck for the forthcoming year. On the first full moon (Daeboreum), which falls on the 15th of the first lunar month, Koreans eat five-grain rice (*ogokbap*), a mixture of any five of the

Left: *Tteokguk* (rice cake soup). It is said you do not turn one year older unless you eat this dish on New Year's Day. Right: *Songpyeon* (half moon-shaped rice cakes). Served on Chuseok, the autumn harvest festival. As the half moon eventually becomes a full moon, the shape reflects hope for a better future.

following: rice, millet, soybeans, red beans, barley, barnyard millet, and sorghum. Also, there is a custom of cracking nuts with one's teeth on this day. This practice is believed to help keep one's teeth healthy for the year. During the Dano festival (the fifth day of the fifth lunar month), which celebrates spring and farming, people eat rice cakes made with mugwort paste. On Chuseok (the harvest festival), one of the biggest holidays in Korea, which takes place on the 15th day of the eighth lunar month under a full moon, people enjoy a variety of traditional foods and special rice cakes such as *songpyeon*. *Songpyeon* are half moon-shaped rice cakes that contain different kinds of sweet or semi-sweet fillings. On the winter solstice (Dongji), people eat porridge made of red beans, called *patjuk*, which is believed to ward off evil spirits.

NUTRITIONAL VALUE OF HOLIDAY FOOD

Korean holiday food includes rice cake soup, dumpling soup, cakes made of glutinous rice, rice cakes steamed on a layer of pine needles, dimes made of five-grain rice, rice gruel prepared with red beans, sweet rice drink, and seasoned dried vegetables. These foods are still very popular with most Koreans.

In addition, nuts are eaten on the fifteenth day of the first lunar month to guard against boils for the year. The nuts include pine nuts, walnuts, peanuts, and chestnuts, and they contain a high concentration of the fatty acid alpha-tocopherol, which is necessary in the cold winter.

Together with the nuts, nine seasoned dried vegetables are eaten on the same day, providing a good supplement of cellulose. The five-grain dishes consist of a mixture of any five of the following: rice, millet, soybeans, red beans, barley, barnyard millet, and sorghum. They contain vitamin B_1, calcium, iron, and cellulose. Beans, especially, are high in protein and thus offer a supplement of amino acids lacking in rice. Boiled rice with other cereals reduces the quantity of sugar in the blood.

Ogokbap (five-grain rice): This dish used to be served at the end of winter on the holiday of Daeboreum. Thanks to its rich nutritional value, it is now popular with increasingly health-conscious Koreans.

Patjuk (red bean porridge): Not only is this a healthy dish, but its red color was once believed to scare away evil spirits.

Such traditions of consuming certain kinds of holiday dishes on different occasions are not the result of personal choice or temporary desire. These traditions evolved quite naturally over a long period of time.

There are good reasons for preparing a specific kind of food at a specific time of the year, and many of the traditions inevitably arose as a result of seasonal and agricultural activities. In summer, when barley and wheat are harvested, boiled barley (instead of rice) and noodles are usually consumed. In autumn, rice and foxtail millet are harvested, so they are the typical ingredients in food eaten in that season. The same applies to the side dishes. In spring, wild mountain greens are eaten as side dishes, while in summer vegetables grown in fields, such as lettuce and cabbage, are consumed.

Nuts were eaten on Daeboreum. It is believed that cracking nuts with your teeth on that day keeps you safe for a year—and keeps your teeth healthy.

KOREAN HOLIDAY FOOD

Until recently, Korea was a primarily agricultural society, so most of its festival customs are tied to farming. Koreans of old used a lunar calendar divided into 24 periods; each period lasted 15 days. Throughout this calendar, there are several festivals during which tasty food is prepared as a sacrificial offering to ancestors and as a meal to share with family and neighbors. This food is called *jeolsik*. The two biggest feast days in the Korean calendar are the autumn harvest holiday of Chuseok and Seollal, the Lunar New Year.

SEOLLAL
(New Year's Day)

- 1st day of 1st month
- *Tteokguk* (rice cake soup), *yakgwa* (honey cakes)

CHOPAIL
(Buddha's Birthday)

- 8th day of 4th month
- Different types of *tteok*, dumplings, special dishes made of fish

DANO
(Celebration of spring and farming)

- 5th day of 5th month
- Varieties of *tteok*, herb rice cakes

JAN FEB MAR APR **MAY** JUN

DAEBOREUM
(First full moon)

- 1st full moon of 1st month
- *Ogokbap* (rice made of five grains), *yaksik* (glutinous rice), *bureom* (nuts)

SAMJINNAL
(Celebrating the coming of spring)

- 3rd day of 3rd month
- *Hwajeon* (rice pancakes), *dugyeonju* (azalea wine)

HANSIK
(Start of farming season)

- 105 days after winter solstice
- Cold food only: *Ssuktteok* (mugwort cake), *ssukdanja* (mugwort dumplings), *ssuktang* (mugwort soup)

YUDU
(Water greeting)

- 15th day of 6th month
- Noodles

CHILSEOK
(Meeting day of Gyeonwoo and Jingnyeo in Korean folk tale)

📅 7th day of 7th month

🍴 *Miljeonbyeong* (wheat pancake), *milguksu* (wheat noodles)

BAEKJUNG
(Time when hundreds of fruits and grains become ripe)

📅 15th day of 7th month

🍴 Food made of potato, flour, and wheat along with a variety of wild vegetables

DONGJI
(Winter solstice)

📅 11th month

🍴 *Patjuk* (Red bean porridge)

JL **AUG** SEP OCT NOV **DEC**

SAMBOK
(Hottest days of the summer)

📅 Between 6th and 7th month

🍴 *Samgyetang* (chicken-ginseng soup), *bosintang* (dog meat soup)

CHUSEOK
(Harvest festival)

📅 15th day of 8th month

🍴 *Songpyeon*, *torantang* (taro soup)

SEOTDAL GEUMEUM
📅 New Year's Eve

🍴 Food for the next day, Seollal

FUNCTIONS OF HOLIDAY DISHES

New Year's Day (Seollal) is about paying respect to ancestors. The 15th of the first lunar month is a day for offering tribute to the village gods, and the Dano festival is a day of wishing for the crops to grow well. Chuseok, in August, is a day for offering the various freshly harvested crops to the gods before consuming them. As such, these special lunar days are unique in the year, occasions for special rituals and games. Taking a rest from everyday work, people hold ancestral memorial services or perform sacrificial rites for the village god, involving the whole village. People put on new clothes, eat delicious holiday food, and visit their relatives and neighbors to exchange greetings. Naturally, the food cannot but be different from everyday food. There are several reasons for preparing a special holiday dish on a traditional holiday.

Ceremonial Need

First, the significance of the holiday can be brought to life and its function indicated by the special food prepared. Holidays such as Seollal and Chuseok are for worshiping ancestors, praying for a rich harvest, or performing exorcisms to prevent tragedies. In order to properly perform these holiday ceremonies, all sorts of food offerings are prepared. On the 15th of the first lunar month, rice with five different grains is served to bring about a bumper crop, and on the winter solstice red beans are cooked and mashed into porridge to drive the ghosts away. In order to bring the tradition of the holiday alive, a dish appropriate to the occasion is necessary.

Nutritional Supplement

Second, by making and eating a holiday dish with the crops and greens grown in the given season, the consumers receive a supplement of nutrients not obtained from everyday food. All foods are most nutritious when consumed during the season in which they are harvested. Accordingly, holiday food helps us to stay healthy. For instance, there's the eating of rice cakes made of mugwort paste during the Dano festival. Mugwort is a wild green plant known to give one energy; it is widely used as a precious herb in traditional Oriental medicine. It is also said that its effects are best during the Dano festival. Therefore, it is customary to pick mugwort during the Dano festival, dry it to make medicine, and use its tender leaves to make rice cakes. By observing the traditions of eating freshly harvested rice on Chuseok, making rice cakes and rice wine to go with it, and consuming various kinds of fresh autumn fruits and vegetables, Koreans eat every kind of food grown in autumn.

Revitalizing Daily Life

Third, by eating delicious food that is not usually eaten and that is reserved for that day, one can enjoy the holiday in a festive mood. Traditional holidays provide relief from the tedious daily chores of life and revitalize us. Good clothes that are not usually worn on ordinary days are put on, games are played, and delicious food is consumed. In this way, the holiday is truly enjoyed. The delicious food and rice wine offered at weddings and on other special occasions also heighten the festive mood and make the day feel special. Various kinds of rice cakes and wine, fruit, and meat are prepared in addition to rice.

Pungmulnori, a rural dance almost universal to Korea's farm villages.

Charyesang:
Table Setting for Ancestral Rites

One of the most important of Korea's traditional rites, Korea's Confucian ancestral rite required the preparation of much ancestral food, the table placement of which followed strict rules handed down over generations.

On the table prepared for an ancestral ceremony on Lunar New Year, the ancestral tablet is placed to the north. The dishes, meanwhile, are usually placed in five rows. Instead of rice, rice cake soup is served.

On the first row is placed a wine glass and rice cake soup. The soup is placed on the left and the wine glass on the right. The chopsticks and a plate are placed in the middle.

The second row contains fried foods. From left to right are fried meats, fried seafood, and fried tofu and vegetables. With fish, the head faces the east and the tail the west.

Stews are placed in the third row. Meat stews are placed on the left, vegetable and tofu stews in the middle, and fish stews on the right.

In the fourth row are the side dishes. Dried seafood is placed at the left end, followed by vegetables, soy sauce, and kimchi, with *sikhye* (rice punch) or *sugeonggwa* (persimmon punch) placed at the right end. The only form of kimchi served is water kimchi made from radish.

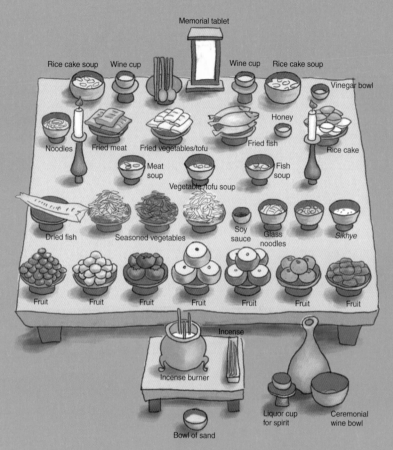

Memorial tablet

Rice cake soup — Wine cup — Wine cup — Rice cake soup — Vinegar bowl

Honey

Noodles — Fried meat — Fried vegetables/tofu — Fried fish — Rice cake

Meat soup — Fish soup

Vegetable/tofu soup

Dried fish — Seasoned vegetables — Soy sauce — Glass noodles — *Sikhye*

Fruit — Fruit — Fruit — Fruit — Fruit — Fruit — Fruit

Incense

Incense burner

Bowl of sand

Liquor cup for spirit — Ceremonial wine bowl

   On the fifth row, fruit is placed. Fruits are always placed in odd numbers. Red fruits are placed to the east, while white fruits are placed to the west. From left to right, there are jujubes, chestnuts, pears, and persimmon.

   When preparing a table for ancestral rites, first the utensils and plates are put on the table, while the incense burner is placed on a small table in front of the food table. Underneath that table is a small bowl of ceremonial wine and a bowl with sand, into which the liquor is poured. When preparing food for an ancestral rite, no red chili pepper powder or garlic is used.

CEREMONIAL FOOD

Being born into this world has always been considered an act of grace and a mystical phenomenon. The belief that humans are born into the world by divine will was common in ancient times because people wanted an explanation for the mystery. Korea was no exception. Through the inculcation of a divine dimension, human life came to be regarded as very precious. Accordingly, people marked special events and gave them special meaning.

From the time one is born to the day one dies, he or she must pass through several noteworthy rites of passage. These rites of passage are accompanied by special dishes. Korea has been part of the Confucian cultural zone from early on, so the influence of Confucianism is felt in all parts of Korean life. In Confucian cultures, rites of passage and ceremonies are considered very important. Some important ceremonies include coming-of-age rites, weddings, funerals, and ancestral rites.

Tables for rites of passage include ones for happy events, beginning with the Samsinsang (prepared before birth to pray for a smooth delivery), *baegilsang* (for the first 100 days), *dolsang* (for the first

Doljabi: This custom, held on a baby's first birthday, is said to determine the future of the child.

birthday), *gwallyesang* (for the coming-of-age), *hollyesang* (for weddings), *keunsang* (for guests of honor), and *hoegapsang* (for 60th birthdays), as well as ones for ancestral ceremonies like the *jesa* and *charye* (see p86).

Given the importance Confucianism places on filial piety, ancestral ceremonies were strictly observed, and the preparation of the table was carried out with great care and attention to long-established rules and traditions.

Birth

Just before delivery, three bowls of rice and three bowls of soup are set on a table. Helpers rub their hands in supplication to Samsin or Sansin, the goddess of childbirth, who governs pregnancy, safe birth, and child rearing. Samsin is also called Samsirang or Samsin *halmeoni* (Grandmother Samsin) depending on the region. The table for Samsin includes plain white rice, seaweed soup, and water drawn from a well

Miyeok guk, seaweed soup

at daybreak. Then, someone, usually the grandmother, prays for the mother's health and the baby's longevity, rubbing her hands while she recites. After a woman has delivered her baby, plain white rice and seaweed soup are served to her.

On the third day after delivery, the mother washes herself with boiled sagebrush water and washes the baby with warm water for the first time. Three bowls of plain white rice and three bowls of seaweed soup are prepared and set on a table for Samsin, and again a prayer is recited. It is only from this third day that others can see the newborn.

Baegil (100th Day)

The hundredth day after the delivery is called *baegil* and a special ceremonial feast is held to celebrate. In the morning, plain white rice and seaweed soup are prepared for Samsin, and a prayer is recited for the last time. After the mother has eaten the rice and soup, the food for the banquet is arranged on a table.

Different kinds of rice cakes are served for *baegil*: steamed rice cakes, which represent purity and cleanliness; glutinous kaoliang rice cakes and glutinous rice cakes coated with mashed red beans, which represent endurance and strong will; rice cakes steamed on a layer of pine needles, which represent generosity; and stuffed rice cakes, which represent the full mind. Each cake is made for longevity, purity, and divinity. It is important that at least one hundred people partake of the cakes so that the baby will enjoy a long life.

The neighbors and relatives should in turn present rice and string, as they represent longevity and good fortune. The *baegil* party is to bless the baby and to prevent any disasters that may hinder the baby's growth.

Doljanchi

The first birthday party is called *doljanchi* and is more elaborate than the *baegil* party. The main foods served are rice cakes and fruits. The same four kinds of rice cakes as for *baegil* are prepared, especially the steamed rice cake and the glutinous rice cake. Other cakes of cinnamon bark and steamed rice balls rolled in various colored powders or steamed in different layers are also served. This steamed layered cake, called *mujigae tteok* (rainbow rice cake), is made in the hope that the baby will have a wide range of accomplishments, as varied as the colors of a rainbow.

One special custom observed during the *doljanchi* is the *doljabi*. On a table, various items are spread out, such as rice, rice cakes, cookies, money, thread, books, paper, a writing brush, and a bow and arrow. For girls, a pair of scissors and a ruler take the place of the bow and arrow. The baby is formally dressed in traditional costume and encouraged to take hold of anything he or she likes. According to the item, the baby's future is

Mujigae tteok, rainbow rice cake

foretold. Money or rice indicates future wealth. Thread represents longevity, and books or a brush represent scholarship.

The *dol* food is also shared with relatives and neighbors, who usually give presents with blessings. The presents include thread, clothing, money, rings, spoons and chopsticks, bowls, and toys.

Every birthday is celebrated by sharing food with relatives and neighbors. As in the case of *baegil* and *dol*, tables for Samsin and for the god who takes care of the house are prepared in the main living room, and prayers are offered for longevity and good fortune. The person celebrating his or her birthday eats the food placed on the table for Samsin.

Coming-of-Age

According to the *Yeseo* (the Book of Etiquette), the coming-of-age ceremony is held between the ages of fifteen and twenty for boys and at fifteen for girls. For boys, the parents must not have lost any of their parents or close senior relatives during the previous year; otherwise, the ceremony is postponed. Traditionally, Korean boys of fifteen years were supposed to have a knowledge of the *Analects* of Confucius and the *Book of Filial Piety*. At this age, the boy is

Traditional coming-of-age ceremony

expected to understand the proper manners, ways, and teachings of the sages. It was considered important that the ceremony be performed after the boy had learned these things.

The ceremony is usually held in the first month of the lunar calendar. Three days before the ceremony, the master of the family announces the event to the family's ancestral tablet hall and chooses the officiator of the ceremony.

The food for the ceremonial table includes wine, dried spiced meat, and boiled meat, all of which is relatively simple. But other food such as noodles, rice cakes, other meat, wine, and fruits are prepared for relatives and visitors.

Weddings

Traditionally, marriage can only take place when the couple has been recognized and accepted as suitable by the families. This is considered extremely important: not only do the two individuals marry, but the two families are also brought together in a close and lasting relationship.

In traditional Korean society, the act of marriage consists of four separate processes and is based on the book *Inquiry into the Four Ceremonies*.

The agreement to marry is the first step in the marriage process. The right ages for marriage as prescribed in the book *Etiquette* are between sixteen and thirty for boys and between fourteen and twenty for girls. At first, the views of both families are communicated through a matchmaker. Only after the girl's family agrees to the marriage can those involved move on to the second step.

When both families agree to the marriage, the family of the boy sends a letter proposing the marriage to the girl's family, along with another letter in which the *saju* ("four pillars," the year, month, day, and hour of birth) of the bridegroom-to-be are written. This letter is folded in five, and the *saju* are written in the middle. The letter is put in an envelope on which the *saju* characters are written. Then the envelope is sealed, wrapped in a cloth, and sent to the girl's family by the matchmaker.

Weddings were held in the bride's yard or house. The groom traveled by horse to the bride's house and, after the wedding ceremony, took his wife in a palanquin (sedan chair) to his parents' house to live. The bride and groom wore formal court costumes for the wedding ceremony. Ordinary people were permitted to wear the luxurious clothes only on their wedding day. Traditionally, the groom's family would carry a wedding chest filled with gifts for the bride's family. Wedding ducks are a symbol for a long and happy

Traditional wedding ceremony

marriage. Cranes are a symbol of long life and may be represented on the woman's sash.

The presentation of the new bride to the bridegroom's parents for the first time is now called *pyebaek*. The bride offers wine and slices of dried beef or steamed chicken as a side dish. The mother-in-law then casts Chinese dates or chestnuts at the bride, wishing for the prosperity of the offspring of the new couple.

Sixtieth Birthday Anniversaries

A person's sixtieth birthday is called *hoegap*. Celebrations are usually organized by the person's offspring. The banquet is magnificent. The main table, called *mangsang*, is placed in front of the parents, and another big table, the *gyojasang*, is separately prepared for the parents as well. The offspring fill a cup with wine, offer it to the parents, and bow two by two. Meanwhile, there is dancing and music, and a Korean drinking song is sung by invited performers. The senior guests are carefully looked after and served wine and side dishes. The *hoegap* is also called *hwangap*, *hwangapyeon*, or *suyeon*.

Main table for *hoegap*

Funerals

Funerals are the most serious ceremonies because they deal with the dead and their spirits. The funeral ceremony is a complicated process starting from the time of death and continuing for up to two years. After that, there are the yearly memorial ceremonies.

Fixed rules for arranging the offerings must be followed. The tablets should be placed to the north. Close to the tablets, a cup of wine, cooked rice and soup, seasoned meat on skewers, soup again, seasoned vegetables, and fruits are placed.

Facing the table, there are some other rules for the arrangement of offerings on it.

1. Red fruits are placed to the east and white ones to the west.
2. Chinese dates, chestnuts, pears, and persimmons (fresh or dried) are placed, in that order, from west to east in the front row.
3. Skewered fish is placed to the east and skewered meat to the west.
4. Dried slices of meat seasoned with spices are placed to the west and *sikhye* is placed to the east.

Traditional funeral ceremony

Chapter Six

HISTORY OF KOREAN FOOD

Korea started growing cereals from the mid-Neolithic Age and rice from around 2000 BC. Beans were grown right from the beginning of Korean history, along with various cereals, including rice. As a result, rice, beans, and other cereals became the staples of the Korean diet. Among the various cereals, foxtail (Italian) millet, Chinese millet, and kaoliang (African millet) were grown from the cereal farming period. Barley was introduced only after rice farming began, and wheat much later, around the 1st or 2nd century.

Since the Korean Peninsula is surrounded by sea on three sides, with an intersection of cold and warm currents, and has plenty of large rivers, it is blessed with an abundant supply of seafood. Because of severe seasonal changes, skills in processing fermented food such as *jeotgal* (salted seafood) developed from early times. In addition, Koreans were skillful hunters and established a tradition, rarely seen in agrarian societies, of preparing meat dishes.

Under such circumstances, the ordinary, everyday diet of rice, soup, and shared side dishes evolved. The table setting showed a clear distinction between the main and the subsidiary dishes. It became customary to offer a table set with all sorts of appetizers— drinks, noodle soup flavored with soy sauce, cold noodles, rice cakes, honeyed pastries, and beverages—at rituals and festivals. With four clearly distinct seasons, the foods produced in each region varied greatly, as could be seen in the side dishes consumed on a daily basis. Processed food that could be preserved, such as soy sauce, kimchi, *jeotgal*, and pickled slices of radish and cucumber, was also consumed from ancient times.

Early on, the tradition of preparing special holiday food became popular. This tradition reminded people of holidays and of the need to devote themselves to farming in ordinary times. It also fostered solidarity and harmony between the village residents and family members through a spirit of cooperation.

All of this developed over time through a process of trial and error and finally refinement. The history of a dietary culture is, in many ways, the history of a people. And Korea's dietary culture has certainly enjoyed a unique evolution.

Pottery unearthed in northwest Korea. This shows that in the Neolithic Age, life on the Korean Peninsula switched from hunting and gathering to agriculture.

PALEOLITHIC BEGINNINGS

There are archaeological artifacts from the Lower Paleolithic era (from about 600,000 years ago) at Jeongok-ri in Yeoncheon, Gyeonggi-do; Durubong in Cheongwon, Chungcheongbuk-do; and Simgok-ri in Myeongju, Gangwon-do. In addition, artifacts from the Middle and Upper Paleolithic ages can be found throughout Korea. The artifacts discovered include hand axes, chopping tools, scrapers, rock hammers, and stone knives, which show that early Koreans used fire to cook what they hunted or caught.

As stated previously, Korea began to farm cereals such as foxtail millet, Chinese millet, kaoliang, and barnyard millet from the mid-Neolithic Age and rice from about 2000 BC. Excavations at a historical relic site in the residential area of Jitap-ri, Bongsan-gun, Hwanghae-do, dating back to early 3000 BC, have yielded stone

Various grains produced in Korea (top to bottom, left to right): black rice, soybean, red bean, sorghum, Job's tears, and foxtail millet.

Prehistoric Period on the Korean Peninsula

	Paleolithic Age	Neolithic Age	Bronze Age
Period	About 700,000 years ago	About 8,000 BC	Around 1,000 BC
Tools	Stone and bone tools	Polished stone tools	Bronze
Economic Activity	Nomadic: hunting and gathering	Settlements with agriculture, livestock	Private property
Habitat	Caves, huts	Dugouts	Ground-level housing
Society	Group, egalitarian society	Tribal, egalitarian society	Class society, private property recognized

farming tools, foxtail millet and barnyard millet grains. From the peat bed of Gahyeon-ri, Gimpo-gun in Gyeonggi-do (2100 BC) and the residential area of the 31st Namgyeong Relic of Samseokguyeok in Pyongyang (3000 BC), rice grains have been excavated along with foxtail millet, confirming that rice was grown during this period.

As Korea is situated in the monsoon region of the Temperate Zone, the amount of sun and annual precipitation was just right for rice farming. So rice became the staple of the Korean diet. Though small in area, the Korean Peninsula has an extremely varied climate, so in the regions not quite suited to rice farming, cereals appropriate to the region were grown. This brought about the development of a dietary culture based on the mixing of rice and other cereals.

In order for farming to flourish, there had to be a development in farming tools. In Korea, the Iron Age took place from about 300 to 100 BC, and stone farming tools were replaced by ironware during that period. Tools made of iron have been excavated from Gujeong-ri in Gyeongju-gun, Gyeongsangbuk-do; Yaean-ri in Gimhae, Gyeongsangnam-do; and Wiwon-myeon in Pyeonganbuk -do.

THREE KINGDOMS PERIOD

It was only during the Three Kingdoms period that rice became a staple of the Korean diet. The three kingdoms of Goguryeo (37 BC-AD 668), Baekje (18 BC-AD 660), and Silla (57 BC-AD 935) all engaged in land reformation, expanded irrigation systems, and actively promoted the use of iron farming tools. Rice finally became a staple when the necessary requirements for rice farming (such as cows for tilling) became available and thus contributed to the increase in rice production.

Three Kingdoms Period (5th Century)

Among the three countries, Baekje had the most ideal climate for rice farming, while Silla grew barley and Goguryeo foxtail millet along with rice. It was only in the Unified Silla period (618-935), with the development of tools and the land and the subsequent general increase in rice production, that rice became the main cereal consumed.

Aside from rice, other grains that were grown included barley, wheat, foxtail millet, Chinese millet, beans, red beans, mung beans, African millet, and buckwheat. It was during the middle of the era that Zhang Qian took wheat to China from the western region on the country's border. Around the 4th century, it was introduced to Japan from Korea. Thus it seems likely that wheat was first introduced to Korea around the 1st century with the coming of the Iron Age.

Rice and barley

Barley is thought to have been introduced to Korea earlier than wheat, though the exact date is unknown. After barley was introduced, it was mostly harvested in the southeastern region, and it came to be consumed as a staple together with rice. Though areas such as Pyeongan-do had a relatively ideal climate for growing wheat, it was not produced on a large scale; mostly, it was for family consumption. In the 1930s, the area for wheat farming amounted to only half that of barley nationwide. Wheat has never been consumed as a staple.

Other Developments

There are records showing that Koreans of the Three Kingdoms period raised cows, pigs, chickens, sheep, goats, and ducks and ate eggs. There are even records showing that Baekje people who went to Japan presented the Japanese emperor with milk.

In the 3rd and 4th centuries, Koreans learned to make boats. They built large boats, allowing them to fish in the far-off seas and eat a diversity of fish and sea products. Cooking methods also developed gradually: Koreans could now store wine, sauce, kimchi, and *jeotgal* for a long time, and they diversified their food culture by using syrup, honey, and oil to flavor their food. The typical Korean table setting—with a main dish of grain and vegetables, meat, and fish as side dishes—developed during this period. Due to the development of a royal government, major differences arose in the lifestyles of the ruling class and common folk; accordingly, class differences appeared in eating culture.

GORYEO PERIOD

Food

Goryeo, from the beginning of its foundation, actively implemented farming promotion policies such as distributing land according to rank and giving tax benefits on land newly cleared for farm use. The quantity of rice reserves for emergencies and the price of grains were regulated, too, in order to increase rice production. Naturally, skills in making wine, rice cakes, and rice pastries became highly developed, and making rice wine became a popular custom.

Steamed chestnut rice cakes, steamed mugwort rice cakes, pancakes made with glutinous rice and kaoliang, *tteok sudan* and *yaksik* (glutinous rice mixed with honey, jujubes, and chestnuts) were some of the rice cakes enjoyed during the Goryeo Dynasty. It was during this period that the custom of making red bean porridge on the winter solstice and sharing it with the whole village became popular.

Yaksik

Radish, turnips, lotus roots, taro, leeks, dropwort, lettuce, hollyhock, green onions, water shields, garlic, shallots, cucumbers, and eggplants were cultivated as vegetables during the Goryeo period. Mountain greens and wild mushrooms were consumed as well. High-quality radishes and pears were grown to be made into *chimchae*, or water vegetable kimchi; *chimchae* was fresher than, and the nutrient composition of its vegetables superior to, the fermented vegetables enjoyed during the Three Kingdoms period, and the preservation method was very scientific. Fragrant vegetables, such as lettuce and small green onions, were used for *ssam* (rice or meat wrapped with vegetable leaves), which is one of the simplest, most well-balanced dishes in Korean cuisine.

In the initial period of Goryeo, everyone from the commoners to the king refrained from eating meat due to the influence of Buddhism. The system used for cow slaughtering was very crude, and at one time it was even banned. Therefore, meat dishes were not enjoyed until the mid-Goryeo Dynasty when high-quality cattle were raised on Jeju Island ranches; meat dishes were then restored and developed. Among the famous meat dishes of the Goryeo Dynasty were *seolya myeokjeok* (roasted prime ribs) and *seolleongtang* (bone and tripe soup). In addition to beef, other meats that were consumed included pork, lamb, chicken, pheasant, and swan.

Drinks and Sweets

During the Goryeo Dynasty, the culture of tea reached its peak. A tea village was formed near Mt. Jirisan to grow tea leaves, and high -quality tea was imported from Song China. There was a tea chamber at the court for brewing tea, and during national ceremonies such as Yeondeunghoe (a light festival on the 15th of the first lunar month, where one offers one's wishes to the Buddha) and Palgwanhoe (ritual ceremonies held for local gods), tea rituals were performed and refreshments prepared.

Along with the tea culture, pastries became highly developed. Pastries can be largely divided into *yumilgwa* (fried honey cookies), *yugwa* (fried cookies made from glutinous rice), *dasik* (small cakes eaten with green tea), *jeonggwa* (candied fruit), and *gwapyeon* (jellied fruit) (see p41). Among these various types, *yumilgwa* was most popular during the Goryeo Dynasty. *Yumilgwa* were served at wedding feasts, and tea with *yumilgwa* was used for entertaining guests. Noodles developed into a food for festive occasions, and *sanghwa*—steamed wheat-flour buns—were first brought from China during the Yuan Dynasty and subsequently became very popular.

Goryeo porcelain wine bottle

The rice wine enjoyed during the Goryeo Dynasty can be divided into *cheongju* (clear strained rice wine) and *beopju* (wine made according to certain rules). When *soju* was introduced during the late Goryeo Dynasty, distilled drinks began to gain popularity. Breweries developed during this period, and countless varieties of rice wine, such as *podoju* (grape wine), *changpoju* (iris wine), *hwanggukju* (chrysanthemum wine), *jukyeopju* (bamboo leaf wine), and *ogapiju* (root bark wine), were consumed.

The Coming of the Mongols and the Return of Meat

In the latter part of the Goryeo era, the military grew more powerful than the monks; with the resulting change in social mores, meat came back into fashion. The invasion of the Mongols and resulting cultural exchange with the Yuan Dynasty brought to Korea imports like sugar, black pepper, and grape wine. During the period of Mongol domination in the later Goryeo era, Koreans learned slaughtering practices and meat preparation. In fact, Korea's meat culture owes a lot to influence from the Yuan Dynasty. Dishes like *gomtang*, *pyeonyuk* (see p34), and *sundae* are nearly identical to similar dishes from the Yuan Dynasty.

Gaeseong Cuisine

The Goryeo capital of Gaeseong was the economic and cultural capital of Korea and developed a unique, splendid palace cuisine. To this day, Gaeseong is renowned for having one of Korea's top three regional cuisines, along with Seoul and the Jeolla-do region. Representative dishes include *bossam* kimchi (wrapped kimchi),

Seolleongtang

pyeonsu (summer *mandu* in a square shape), *sinseollo* (royal casserole), *seolleongtang* (beef tripe soup), *chueotang* (mudfish soup), *joraengi tteokguk* (rice cake soup), *umegi* (*tteok* covered with syrup), and *gyeongdan* (ball-shaped *tteok*).

From the records on cuisine from the period, we can see that its elite had a highly developed culinary culture. The Goryeo era was when Korean cooking came into its own, with food and seasonings diversifying.

JOSEON PERIOD

In the early Joseon era, there was little change in the food culture from the Goryeo era. From the 16th century, however, Confucian culture matured and *yangban* culture took root, which would have a major impact on the culinary culture. Due to the impact of Confucianism, a patriarchal social system was established, with an emphasis on rites. Based on the teachings of the Chinese philosopher Zhu Xi, rites like marriage, funerals, and ancestral ceremonies were codified and strictly kept. Among Korea, China, and Japan, only Korea continues to adhere to the practice of using chopsticks and a spoon. This was because they used a spoon in the

Paddy field

time of Confucius, and Korea's Confucianists kept the practice to the end.

The food culture of Joseon grew more diverse, and *yangban* homes produced books documenting cooking and brewing methods, while special foods were served during holidays. Regional cuisines developed during this period, too.

Agricultural Technique Development

From the Joseon Dynasty, agricultural techniques became more developed and the types of grains cultivated more varied. From the beginning of the Joseon Dynasty, practical farming textbooks such as *Nongsa Jikseol* were written. They contributed greatly to the development of farming techniques appropriate to Korea. From that time on, many farming books, such as *Pangye Surok*, were published, bringing agricultural development to the whole peninsula. From the mid-Joseon Dynasty, irrigation was extended, and rice planting methods were followed on a national scale. With this, the planting of rice and barley became easier, and cows began to be widely used in farming. Among the grains grown during this period were 69 kinds of rice, 15 kinds of foxtail millet, eight kinds of bean, seven kinds of red bean, and four kinds of barley, among others. Cowpeas, peas, buckwheat, and corn—which had been introduced in the 18th century—were also grown.

Foreign Foods Introduced

It was also during the Joseon Dynasty that chili peppers, pumpkins, potatoes, sweet potatoes, tomatoes, and other foreign foods were first introduced. Chili peppers and pumpkins are thought to have been brought in from Japan before or after the Japanese invasion of Korea in 1592, but in Japan there is a belief that the chili pepper was brought from Korea. In any event, the chili peppers grown on the Korean Peninsula, unlike the ones that were originally introduced, were uniquely sweet and hot (a mixture of chili and paprika), and this contributed greatly to the development of the particular taste that is most characteristic of Korea's traditional food. In particular, with the use of red chili pepper and *jeotgal* in kimchi, the dish really came into its own as a tasty and nutritious fermented food.

Seafood and Meat

Fishing techniques were further refined, and due to the increase in sea produce during the Joseon Dynasty and the development of the barter economy, fisheries started to be managed on a large scale. As a result, the production of seafood showed a rapid increase. The principal catches of large-scale fishing during this period were croakers, herrings, codfish, and anchovies. After seaweed and sea tangle—popular local produce from antiquity—sea laver began to be cultivated as a major product as well. Laver was raised on Wando Island, Jeolla-do, from the mid-Joseon Dynasty. The sea produce was dried, processed in salt water or fermented, and supplied on a nationwide scale. The most famous sea produce is Alaskan pollack, which is considered to be of the best quality when it is dried in January. Around the 17th century, some 140 different kinds of *jeotgal* were consumed, including fermented croaker,

Myeongtae (pollack) is Korea's most typical seafood product. Depending on how it is caught and processed, it is called by many names. Unfrozen, it is called *saengtae*; dried, it is called *bugeo*; half-dried, it is called *kodari*; caught in winter and frozen, it is called *dongtae*; caught in the breeding season and frozen and dried repeatedly, it is called *hwangtae*. Young *myeongtae* are called *nogari*, while *myeongtae* eggs are fermented to make *myeongnanjeot*.

salted dry croaker, salted oysters with chili pepper, and fermented flatfish with rice punch.

Beef, pheasant, chicken, and pork were also widely eaten. The beef raised on Jeju-do was especially tasty and noted for its high quality. Also, roe deer, deer and bear's feet were considered culinary delicacies. The usual way of preparing these meals was to make beef jerky, *gui* (roasts), *jjim* (steamed food), *gomtang* (beef soup), or jelly.

Food Culture in the Joseon Period

During the Joseon Dynasty, a strictly patriarchal and extended family structure began to take root in society, due to the influence of Confucianism, the political and moral standard of the time. Along with this, the norms of traditional rituals and ceremonial occasions (coming-of-age, marriages, funerals, and ancestral memorial ceremonies) were carefully observed. Naturally, the norms concerning food in each of these ceremonies were rigid and strict. And since the family structure was an extended one, with several generations living under the same roof, managing the food became a major affair.

The procurement of food and its processing, cooking, and distribution were the sole responsibility of the housewife. Not only that, but preparing breakfast at dawn for the elders, procuring home-brewed liquor, cooking side dishes, and stocking soy sauce, pastes, and fermented foods were considered very important. A unique tradition of making holiday and seasonal food to provide supplementary nutrition in each season, as well as to wish for a good harvest and consolidate harmony within the family and the village, came to be observed. Also developing during this period was palace cuisine, making use of high-quality ingredients brought together by palace cooks trained in the highest cooking methods. The late Joseon era was the golden age of Korean cuisine, when it experienced its greatest development.

Chapter Seven

THE KITCHEN

The kitchen is one of the most important areas in a house. Not only is it important for cooking and heating the house, but historically it was always the place where the grains were pounded in a mortar and where the women and girls washed themselves at the end of a long hard day. The younger members of the family had their meals in the kitchen, daughters-in-law cried out their tears of frustration and anguish there, and many used the poker instead of a brush as they tried to educate themselves. Therefore, the kitchen was not only a kitchen. It was a bathing room, a resting place, a school, and the center of family life in traditional Korean society. For the newly married daughter-in-law, it was her place of employment, where, for twenty or thirty years from the third day of marriage, she had to go in and out from morning till night. In fact, women spent most of their lives in the kitchen, and the housekeeping and organization of the family took place there.

THE FIREPLACE

The most important and sacred place in the kitchen has always been the fireplace. Housewives tried hard to keep the fireplace clean at all times, and the degree of its cleanliness was the measure of their abilities. Jowang, the kitchen god, was considered to reside in a small bowl of water kept on a shelf in the center of the wall behind the fireplace. The housewife changed the water in the bowl each day with water freshly drawn from the well at daybreak and prayed for the well-being and happiness of the family for that day.

Jowang was considered in some places to reside in various other things, including a gourd dipper fitted with a piece of hemp on a lathe; a piece of white paper or white cloth pasted to the wall; a piece of folded paper with a piece of dried pollack pasted to the wall; a small jar filled with rice behind a kettle; or a kettle on the cooking fireplace. In the last case, people would pray at the shrine for an easy delivery when a birth was drawing near.

Agungi, the Korean traditional fireplace

THE KITCHEN GOD

Jowang is believed to go up to the heavens on the 23rd day of the 12th lunar month. There, Jowang precisely informs the heavens of all the affairs of the house for the year until his return at daybreak on New Year's Day. Therefore, if a person has committed any wrong, he or she must stick rice gluten over the mouth of the fireplace on the night before Jowang ascends. The mouth of the fireplace symbolizes the way that Jowang passes to the heavens, as well as Jowang's mouth. As it is sealed with rice gluten, Jowang has difficulty in rising up to the heavens, and even if he does manage the journey he cannot report anything because his mouth is sealed.

In the kitchens of Korean temples, unlike those of ordinary houses, a statue of Jowang is kept on the shelf above the fireplace, and food is served to it every morning and evening, a custom probably introduced from China. Not all temples have a statue, however. Some have a piece of writing as a substitute.

Traditionally, during the 14th evening of the first lunar month people stole the soil from the yards of the rich and applied it to their cooking fireplace the next day. This was called "stealing the soil of fortune." It was believed that this soil would increase the good fortune of the family in the coming year. The family from whom the soil was stolen was considered to suffer a decrease in fortune. Therefore, on that particular night rich families had special guards posted to prevent anyone from stealing their soil. A similar custom is found in the old texts *Various Events of the Capital* and *Korean Almanac*. There, it is written that people from Seoul dug the soil out of Jongno and either sprinkled some in the four corners of their house or applied it to the cooking fireplace.

Such customs are rooted in the fact that everything grows from the earth. In addition, applying special soil to the fireplace was a way of showing respect and honoring the place where the cooking was done. Not only was this special place honored by applying new soil, but the sections that had been chipped or cracked through wear and tear were also repaired.

KITCHEN UTENSILS

The most representative kitchen utensil is the kettle, or *sot*. Made of iron with a ridge around the center of the body and a lid with a handle, the *sot* has different names according to size. The smallest *sot* was called *ongsot*, the next *jungsot*, followed by *gamasot* and *dumeongsot*.

The *dumeongsot* has a larger mouth and is used to steam or boil large quantities of food for parties. The lid is made of two pieces of wood, shaped like half moons so that it is easy to open and close. The *gamasot* is sometimes used for cooking rice, but it was mainly used for boiling chopped hay for cattle. The *jungsot* and *ongsot* are used for cooking rice and soup, respectively.

A good Korean kettle rings true like a fine earthenware pot. If the sound is unclear, then the iron used is of poor quality or the kettle is cracked. In order to polish the kettle, water is boiled two or three times in it over a weak fire, and then it is rubbed, inside and out, with the fat remaining in the pan after cooking greasy meat. After that, water is once again boiled three or more times in order to rinse the kettle. If this is done, the kettle lasts for a long time and can be used constantly. Another way of preserving the *sot* was to rub some of the soot from the bottom of the kettle on the outside and lid with an oily cloth.

The *sot* is a symbol of good housekeeping. When a house was newly built or a family moved, putting the *sot* on the fireplace was considered to mark the beginning of housekeeping. There are Korean sayings that encapsulate the value and importance of the *sot*; expressions such as "It's been three years since the *sot* was removed from the fireplace" or "just waiting after washing the *sot*" are used to indicate irresolute people. When a family received a new bride into the family, a kettle furnace was built on the threshold of the main room, and the lid of the *jungsot* was placed in front of the doorstep upside down. Then the bride stepped over the lid with her left foot. This symbolized the wish that the bride would be "as healthy as iron and without any troubles." It was also a way to review this new person who would be doing all the cooking in the future.

The *sot* was also believed to foretell coming disasters. If, during the cooking, the *sot* made a "bu-ung, bu-ung" noise or the lid moved up and down to release the steam, these were considered bad omens. If it was the rice kettle that made a noise, the master of the house would enter the kitchen and his wife would bow to him. If, on the other hand, the soup kettle made a noise, then the husband had to bow to his wife until the sound stopped.

Like the thread that accompanies a needle, the *jugeok*, a big fat wooden spoon, accompanies the *sot*. The *jugeok* is used to ladle the

Gamasot

rice out of the *sot* into the bowls. The mate of the *jugeok* is the *gukja*, the soup ladle. The center is concave, and it has a long handle so that hot soup can be ladled easily. In the Neolithic Age, a big shell was used for a ladle. As soup became more and more important during the Goryeo Dynasty, the ladle became essential. Originally made of brass, in later times the ladle was made of albata. Nowadays, stainless steel or synthetic resin is largely used. Since 80% of Korean food falls in the category of soups, the ladle will continue to be an important utensil. Traditionally, the word for soup was used to refer to money or pay. Expressions such as "there is no soup" and "it is a position with no soup" were common.

The *jori*, or bamboo strainer, was used to sift sand out of the rice. Made of fine slips of bamboo woven together to form a mesh, it was moved back and forth in a special way through the rice so that only the grains were caught and the sand left behind. The heavier stones sank to the bottom and so were easily removed. As *jori* separates the good from the bad, it has always symbolized good fortune. A pair of *jori* were often hung diagonally next to each other on doors or on the walls of the main room. The geomantic

theory followed superstition. Thus, land shaped like a *jori* was believed to bring wealth to the people who lived there. On the fourteenth night of the first month, merchants sold *jori* tied with red string. These were called *bok jori* ("good luck *jori*"). The custom was to pay the merchant whatever he

Bok jori

asked without haggling; a discount was believed to lower the amount of good fortune received.

When there was no municipal water system, people drew water from a well and kept it in the *dumeong*, a big jar located near the fireplace. It was usually made of pottery glazed dark brown, but rich families had *dumeong* made of iron. Both had to be well polished and spotlessly clean.

The *siru* was used for steaming rice or rice cakes. The many holes in the bottom allowed the steam to rise up and cook the rice or cakes. The oldest Korean *siru* was found in a shell heap in Chodo in Hamgyeongbuk-do, a site of Bronze Age remains. This proves that the *siru* has been used since the earliest times when primitive farming was just starting. Until recently, two or three *siru* were essential in every household. The rice cakes cooked in *siru* were the best for memorial ceremonies, parties, and festivals. No ceremony was conceivable without rice cakes. In the harvest month, the tenth lunar month, when offerings were made to the spirits, both rice cakes and *siru* were offered. The small *siru* is called an *ongsiru*. At temples or shrines, unbreakable brass *siru* were substituted for earthenware ones. Recently, aluminum *siru* have become very popular. The Korean *siru* was introduced to Japan, where it is called *seiro*, derived from the Korean word.

An iron grilling pan, or *beoncheol*, was used to prepare grilled dishes. Also called a *jeokja* or *jeoncheol*, it is shaped like a Korean kettle, wide and round. There are handles on both sides to make it easy to put on and lift off the fire. When there was a lot of food to grill for a special gathering or party, the lid of the kettle was turned upside down and used for grilling. It is likely that

Siru

the *beoncheol* has been used in Korean kitchens since the time of the Three Kingdoms, when iron kettles were also used. When the pan needed to be oiled, hard vegetables like radishes or potatoes were used to brush the oil on.

Mainly used for water, the gourd dipper, or *bagaji*, was another essential implement in the Korean kitchen. It was made by cutting a gourd in half, scooping out the inside, and drying the shell. The *bagaji* was also used to scoop uncooked raw rice, soya, or bean paste. Another kind of dipper, made of hollowed wood with a short handle, was used to ladle out cattle feed consisting of boiled straw and beans. Gourd dippers have been replaced with plastic ones, and even in rural villages the gourd dipper is rare these days.

The *ttukbaegi* is a small, glazed earthenware bowl used for boiling or stewing. It has a wide mouth, is relatively deep, and is used mainly for making stews with *doenjang* as a main ingredient.

Korean housewives spent much time waiting for their husbands. As they waited, they would place the *ttukbaegi* on and off the stove, trying to keep the food hot and ready for the moment the husband returned. This was a sign of their love and care for their husbands. The *ttukbaegi* is rough and ill-finished, so when the content of something is better than its looks, people say, "*Doenjang* tastes better than a *ttukbaegi* looks." Music

Bagaji, hanging on the wall

that is ugly or out of tune is compared to "the sound of a *ttukbaegi* breaking."

A *che* is used to sift powder or liquid and comes in different sizes. The *che* was also used to drive away misfortune. It was believed that on the 15th of the first lunar month, a luminous ghost came down from the heavens. If the ghost found a child's shoes that fit, it would take the shoes, and the owner would be expected to have bad luck for the following year. In order to prevent the ghost from taking the shoes, a strainer was hung on the outside wall of the house. It was believed that the ghost would be so busy counting the holes in the strainer that time would pass and daybreak would frighten it away.

Certain houses had their own noodle machines. Kneaded dough was placed in the machine; the handle was pressed down, and noodles came out. Noodles were often served at parties or during festivals. Therefore, "eating noodles" means getting married. Noodles were also prepared on birthdays as a symbol of long life.

Some houses had a machine for distilling spirits, and some for pressing oil. As time passed, many utensils became less frequently used and difficult to find. Traditionally, however, everything was prepared in the house, and it was always well equipped with the necessary utensils.

Che (bottom right)

OTHER FUNCTIONS OF THE KITCHEN

In the early days, no house—not even those of the well-to-do—had a separate bathing room. Traditionally, it was considered rude and against accepted etiquette. Therefore, aristocratic men hardly ever took a bath because they were reluctant to remove their clothes in front of others.

Women, on the other hand, used to lock the door and wash themselves in the kitchen using the heated water from the kettle. The kitchen was also a refuge for the daughters-in-law who had to suffer under the strictness of their mothers-in-law and the moodiness of their sisters-in-law. Crouching in front of the fireplace and feeding the fire was a way to rest and recuperate. Sometimes, when the stress was too much, these poor women would break the poker in frustration as they fed the fire.

Being hungry to learn and acquire knowledge, women learned *hangeul*, the Korean alphabet, in the kitchen. They practiced with the poker in the ashes, pretending that it was a calligraphy brush. For it was difficult to study during such a busy life, and those who did could only acquire knowledge in the kitchen.

APPENDIX

OTHER INFORMATION

MORE ABOUT KOREAN FOOD

BOOKS

With Korean cuisine enjoying increasing popularity overseas, you can find a number of books on Korean food and cooking, including cookbooks for those who'd like to explore the world of Korean food in the comfort of their own kitchen.

- Chang, Sun-Young. *A Korean Mother's Cooking Notes*. Seoul: Ewha Womans University Press, 1997.

- Chung, Haekyung. *Korean Cuisine: A Cultural Journey*. Seoul: Thinking Tree, 2009.

- Dong-A Ilbo. *Korean Food, The Originality + Korean Food, The Impression*. Seoul: Dong-A Ilbo Publication, 2010.

- Hepinstall, Hisoo Shin. *Growing Up in a Korean Kitchen: A Cookbook*. Berkeley, California: Ten Speed Press, 2001.

- Institute of Traditional Korean Food. *The Beauty of Korean Food: With 100 Best-Loved Recipes*. Seoul: Hollym, 2008.

- Lee, Cecilia Hae-Jin. *Eating Korean: From Barbecue to Kimchi, Recipes from*

My Home. Hoboken, New Jersey: Wiley, 2005.

- Lee, Cecilia Hae-Jin. *Quick and Easy Korean Cooking*. San Francisco: Chronicle Books, 2009.

- Kim, Yun-sik. *Temple Food to Eat with Your Eyes*. Seoul: Seoul Selection. 2009.

- Kwak, Jenny and Fried, Liz. *Dok Suni: Recipes from My Mother's Korean Kitchen*. New York: St. Martin's Press, 1998.

- Samuels, Debra and Chung, Taekyung. *The Korean Table: From Barbecue to Bibimbap—100 Easy-to-Prepare Recipes*. Singapore: Tuttle Publishing, 2008.

ONLINE RESOURCES

- **Koreataste** www.koreataste.org
Run by the Korea Tourism Organization, this attractive website features restaurant reviews, introductions to Korean dishes, and even interviews with noted experts.

- **ZenKimchi Korean Food Journal** www.zenkimchi.com
Lots of restaurant reviews, recipes, and commentary, as well as a guide to Korean food.

- **Seoul Eats** www.seouleats.com
Run by Daniel Gray, a "food loving Delawarean who came to Korea," the blog focuses on restaurant reviews, but Dan runs a variety of food tour and cooking classes, too.

- **Maangchi** www.maangchi.com
This blog, created by Korean-born and -raised Emily Kim, features videos of her making Korean food.

- **TriFood** www.trifood.com
TriFood is "committed to providing information about Korea and its delicious and healthy food." And indeed, there are tons of recipes, pictures of dishes, and even a glossary of Korean food.

RECOMMENDED RESTAURANTS

The best way to learn about and experience Korean cuisine is to eat it, of course! Here are some Seoul restaurant selections that will help get you started.

HANJEONGSIK/PALACE CUISINE

Hanjeongsik is a full-course Korean meal featuring rice, soup and a table full of sidedishes. If you'd like to experience Korean traditional cuisine at its most sublime, try Korean royal palace cuisine and eat like a king.

Yongsusan

Goryeo-style royal cuisine served in a beautiful setting. Highly recommended. Located just to the west of Changdeokgung Palace (shop in Samcheong-dong, too).

• **Hours** noon to 3 pm / 6 to 10 pm • **Prices** 38,000 to 125,000 won
• **Getting There** Exit 3, Anguk Station, Line 3. Walk toward Changdeokgung Palace and swing a left. Keep walking untill you see Yongsusan on your left. • **Tel** (02) 732-3019

Goongyeon

Run by a master chef who studied old manuscripts to rediscover proper Korean court cuisine. Reservation required.

• **Hours** noon to 3 pm / 5:30 to 8 pm • **Prices** 30,000 to 92,000 won • **Getting There** Exit 1, Anguk Station, Line 3. Turn right at Anguk Intersection and walk to Jaedong Elementary School. Swing a left at the intersection across from the school.
• **Tel** (02) 3673-1104

Seokparang

Housed in a Joseon-era villa, this lovely eatery specializes in Joseon royal cuisine served on antique ceramics. Located in Buam-dong.

• **Hours** noon to 3 pm / 6 to 10 pm • **Prices** Around 45,000 to 100,000 won
• **Getting There** Exit 3, Gyeongbokgung Station, Line 3. Take bus 0212, 1020, 1711, 7018, or 7022 to Sangmyung University. The restaurant is a Korean-style building near there. • **Tel** (02) 395-2500

Dalhangari

Organic Korean home-style *hanjeongsik* that is tasty and good for you. Located in scenic Samcheong-dong.

• **Hours** 11:30 am to 10 pm • **Prices** Around 25,000 won • **Getting There** Exit 1, Anguk Station, Line 3. Walk along Samcheong-dong Road until you get to the Prime Minister's residence. Dalhangari is in front of it. • **Tel** (02) 733-7902

KOREAN MEAT DISHES

Popular Korean meat dishes include *galbi* (ribs, either beef or pork), *bulgogi* (marinated beef grilled atop an open flame), and *samgyeopsal* (Korean-style bacon). All are popular with foreign diners. The meat is typically eaten wrapped in a lettuce leaf with condiments. NOTE: In Korea, beef is usually more expensive than pork.

Bamboo House

Housed in a stunning Frank Gehry-esque building in the tony Yeoksam-dong neighborhood, this pricey establishment does some of the best Korean barbecue and grill in the country in a multilingual setting.

• **Hours** 11:30 am to 2:30 pm / 5:30 to 10:30 pm • **Prices** 40,000 won and up • **Getting There** Exit 7, Yeoksam Station, Line 2. Walk 10 minutes in the direction of Gyeonbok Apartments (or take a cab—if you're eating here, money is clearly not an issue). • **Tel** (02) 555-6390

Cheolgil Wang Galbisal

Wonderful beef *galbi*, served with outstanding bean paste stew. Very popular with the college crowd near Hongik University.

• **Hours** 24 hours • **Prices** Around 25,000 won • **Getting There** Exit 5, Hongik University Station, Line 2. Walk 20 minutes in the direction of the Sanollim Theater—the restaurant is in the alley across from it. • **Tel** (02) 332-9543

Maple Tree House

Samgyeopsal with a beautiful wooded garden in Samcheong-dong.

• **Hours** 11:30 am to 10 pm • **Prices** Around 30,000 won • **Getting There** Exit 1, Anguk Station, Line 3. Walk about 20 minutes along Samcheong-dong Road—the restaurant is near Korea Banking Institute. • **Tel** (02) 730-7461

BIBIMBAP

This simple dish of rice mixed with seasoned vegetables and red chili pepper sauce is fast becoming an overseas favorite. Even Gwyneth Paltrow likes it. It is served in either a metal/plastic bowl or a stone pot (*dolsot bibimbap*).

Gogung

The southwestern city of Jeonju does the best *bibimbap* in Korea. If you can't get there, though, Gogung in Insa-dong does a pretty good Jeonju *bibimbap*.

• **Hours** 11 am to 9 pm • **Prices** Around 10,000 won • **Getting There** Exit 6, Anguk Station, Line 3. Located in the basement of Ssamziegil in Insa-dong. • **Tel** (02) 736-3211

Bon Bibimbap

The flagship store of this chain does an assortment of bibimbap at reasonable prices.

• **Hours** 9:30 am to 10 pm • **Prices** Under 10,000 won • **Getting There** Exit 3, Jonggak Station, Line 1. Walk toward Tapgol Park. Turn left just before the park. Gogung is right there, across from the park, near the entrance to Insa-dong.
• **Tel** (02) 736-4288

SOUPS AND STEWS

Korea does many tasty soups and stews, including *doenjang jjigae* (soybean paste stew), kimchi *jjigae* (kimchi stew), *sundubu jjigae* (tofu stew), *seolleongtang* (milky beef soup), and *samgyetang* (chicken ginseng soup).

Tobang

This place does standard Korean fare like kimchi *jjigae*, *sundubu jjigae*, and *doenjang jjigae*. Also famous for its marinated crab, which it serves as a side dish.

• **Hours** 10:30 am to 10 pm • **Prices** around 5,000 won • **Getting There** Exit 6, Anguk Station, Line 3. Enter Insa-dong. Tobang is on the left. • **Tel** (02) 735-8156

Toetmarujip Doenjang Yesul

Also in Insa-dong, this very traditional-style place run by poet Park Jung-sik specializes in hearty North Korean-style *doenjang jjigae*. Particularly popular is the *doenjang bibimbap* (rice mixed with vegetables and soybean paste stew).

• **Hours** 10:30 am to 10 pm • **Prices** 10,000 to 20,000 won • **Getting There** Exit 5, Jongno 3-ga Station, Line 5. Enter Insa-dong. Face the Seoho Art Gallery at the Insa-dong Intersection and make a left into the alleyway. • **Tel** (02) 739-5683

Bukchon Gamasot Seolleongtang

This pleasant Bukchon restaurant in a Korean traditional home specializes in *seolleongtang*, but it does a good *manduguk* (dumpling soup) as well as other dishes. Food served on Korean traditional ceramics.

• **Hours** 11 am to 10:30 pm • **Prices** 6,000 to 10,000 won • **Getting There** Exit 1, Anguk Station, Line 3. Located in alley in front of Jeongdok Public Library. • **Tel** (02) 725-7355

Jiho Hanbang Samgyetang

Samgyetang, or "ginseng chicken soup," is a Korean summer specialty. A young chicken is stuffed with rice and boiled in a broth of ginseng, jujube, garlic, and ginger.

• **Hours** 11 am to 10 pm • **Prices** 12,000 to 14,000 won • **Getting There** Exit 2, Mia Samgeori Station, Line 4. Walk 10 minutes to Dongseong Car Inspection. • **Tel** (02) 916-3999

DUMPLINGS AND NOODLES

Korea does a number of unique noodle dishes, including *kalgukgsu* (knife-cut wheat noodles in a rich broth) and *naengmyeon* (chilled buckwheat noodles). *Mandu* (Korean-style dumplings) are also popular.

Myeong-dong Gyoja

A Myeong-dong institution, this popular place is famous for its *kalguksu*. It also does wonderful *bibimguksu* (cold wheat noodles served with a tangy red chili pepper sauce) and *mandu*.

• **Hours** 10:30 am to 9:30 pm • **Prices** Under 10,000 won • **Getting There** Exit 8, Myeong-dong Station, Line 4. Walk about 150 m toward Crown Bakery. • **Tel** (02) 776-5348

Woo Lae Oak

Serving quite possibly the best Pyongyang-style *naengmyeon* outside of North Korea, this legendary eatery also does outstanding meat dishes, but be prepared to spend some money—even the relatively cheap *bulgogi* goes for 28,000 won per serving. You can choose between *mul naengmyeon* (served in a mild, chilled beef broth) or *bibim naengmyeon* (served with spicy red chili pepper sauce).

• **Hours** 11:30 am to 10 pm • **Prices** 10,000 won and up • **Getting There** Exit 4, Euljiro 4-ga Station, Line 5. Turn right at the first alley. • **Tel** (02) 2265-0151

Jaha Son Mandu

This place in lovely Buam-dong does a variety of *mandu* dishes, including *tteokmanduguk* (rice cake soup with dumplings), kimchi *mandu jeongol* (kimchi and dumpling stew), and *pyeonsu* (steamed Gaeseong-style dumplings).

• **Hours** 11 am to 9 pm • **Prices** around 10,000 to 35,000 won • **Getting There** Exit 5, Gyeongbokgung Station, Line 3. Take a taxi from there, as it's a long walk.
• **Tel** (02) 379-2648

VEGETARIAN

Korea probably could not in fairness be called a paradise for vegetarians, but vegetarian food can be found if you know where to look.

Sanchon

Selected by the Asia Wall Street Journal's John Krich as one of the ten best restaurants in Asia in 2007, this Insa-dong institution, run by a Buddhist monk, does vegetarian temple cuisine. Meals come with a bewildering assortment of side dishes, and dinner is accompanied by Korean traditional music and dancing.

• **Hours** 11 am to 10 pm • **Prices** 22,000 won (lunch), 39,600 won (dinner)
• **Getting There** Exit 6, Anguk Station, Line 3. Head down Insa-dong and turn left into the alley at Atelier Seoul. Sanchon is at the end of the alley. • **Tel** (02) 735-0312

Baru (Temple Stay Information Center)

On the fifth floor of the Temple Stay Information Center across the street from Jogyesa Temple, this restaurant serves vegetarian Buddhist temple cuisine, with options for 10-dish, 12-dish and 15-dish courses.

• **Hours** 11 am to 2:30 pm / 5:30 to 9 pm • **Prices** 25,000 to 50,000 won

• **Getting There** Exit 2, Jonggak Station, Line 1. Walk 70 m to Jogyesa Temple. The Temple Stay Information Center is across the street. • **Tel** (02) 2031-2081

QUICK KOREAN EATS

Don't have time for a full meal? There are plenty of places to find low priced, quickly served food like *gimbap* (rice rolls), *ramyeon* (instant noodles), and *tteokbokki* (spicy rice cakes).

Gimbap Cheonguk

Gimbap (rice rolls), *mandu* (dumplings), and noodle dishes. Great for a cheap meal on the go.

• **Hours** 24 hours • **Prices** Under 5,000 won. A chain with shops almost everywhere, this place serves good, cheap Korean fare.

Sindang Tteokbokki Alley

This alleyway near Sindang Station is lined with restaurants doing *tteokbokki*, one of Seoul's signature dishes. Rice cakes pan-fried with a spicy red chili pepper sauce, vegetables, dumplings, and noodles, it's cheap, filling and tasty.

• **Hours** 24 hours • **Prices** 10,000 to 20,000 won

COOKING CLASSES

Want to get your hands dirty? Here are some places to learn Korean cooking:

• **National Palace Museum of Korea** (www.gogung.go.kr)
Located on the grounds of Gyeongbokgung Palace, the National Palace Museum of Korea holds Korean palace cuisine cooking classes.

• **O'ngo Food Communications** (www.ongofood.com)
Started by Jia Choi in 2007, this group offers both tours and cooking classes (beginner, intermediate and advanced).

• **Korea House** (www.kangkoku.or.kr)
Run by the Korea Cultural Heritage Foundation, this beautiful (mostly) *hanok* cultural center on the slope of Mt. Namsan offers basic kimchi and *bulgogi*-making classes.

• **Tteok Museum** (www.kfr.or.kr)
In addition to *tteok* (rice cakes), this museum, run by the Institute of Traditional Korean Food, also offers classes on making kimchi and other Korean traditional foods.

The content of this book has been compiled, edited, and supplemented from the following articles published in:

Koreana Vol. 7, No. 3, Autumn 1993
"History of Korean Dietary Culture" by Yun Seo-seok
"The Scientific Significance of Traditional Korean Food" by An Myung-soo
"Dietary Customs and Their Characteristics" by Kang In-hee
"Life's Milestones: Ceremonies and Food" by Park Tae-sun
"Korean Holidays: Customs and Food" by Yim Jae-hae
"Table Setting and Cookery" by Han Pok-chin
"The Kitchen" by Kim Kwang-on

Koreana Vol. 22, No. 4, Winter 2008
"Ideal Health Food for a Well-Being Lifestyle" by Park Kun-young
"Sharing Kimchi with Consumers Around the World" by Nam Sang-won
"Background and Development of Korean Kimchi" by Jo Jae-sun

PHOTOGRAPHS

Image Today 4, 5, 7, 11, 12, 14-18, 20-23, 25-38, 40, 41, 43-47, 49, 53, 55, 63, 65, 73, 76, 79, 81-83, 85, 86, 91, 95, 98, 101, 102, 104, 106, 108, 111, 112, 115-119, 121, 122
Yonhap Photo 29, 52, 58, 61, 64, 67, 68, 88, 89, 92, 94, 97
Robert Koehler 19, 35, 70
Ryu Seunghoo 65
Ben Jackson 8
US Army photo
By Debbie Hong 33, 105
By Edward N. Johnson 93

(* Presence of U.S. Government media does not imply endorsement.)

CREDITS

Publisher	Kim Hyung-geun
Writer	Robert Koehler
Editor	Lee Jin-hyuk
Copy Editor	Colin A. Mouat
Proof Reader	Ben Jackson
Designer	Jung Hyun-young